Persuasion

Sandra D. Collins

7 Managerial Communication Series | Editor: James S. O'Rourke, IV

SOUTH-WESTERN
CENGAGE Learning™

Australia • Brazil • Japan • Korea • Mexico • Singapore • Spain • United Kingdom • United States

SOUTH-WESTERN
CENGAGE Learning™

Persuasion: Managerial Communication Series
James S. O'Rourke IV, series editor;
Sandra D. Collins

VP/Editorial Director: Jack W. Calhoun

VP/Editor-in-Chief: Melissa Acuńa

Acquisitions Editor: Erin Joyner

Developmental Editor: Daniel Noguera

Marketing Manager: Mike Aliscad

Content Project Manager: Jana Lewis

Manager of Technology, Editorial: John Barans

Technology Project Editor: John Rich

Manufacturing Coordinator: Diane Gibbons

Production Service: Pre-Press PMG

Art Director: Stacy Jenkins Shirley

Internal Designer: Robb & Associates

Cover Designer: Robb & Associates

For product information and technology assistance, contact us at
Cengage Learning Academic Resource Center, 1-800-423-0563

For permission to use material from this text or product,
submit all requests online at **www.cengage.com/permissions**
Further permissions questions can be emailed to
permissionrequest@cengage.com

Library of Congress Control Number: 2007942576

ISBN-13: 978-0-324-58421-9

ISBN-10: 0-324-58421-0

South-Western Cengage Learning
5191 Natorp Boulevard
Mason, OH 45040
USA

Cengage Learning is a leading provider of customized learning solutions with office locations around the globe, including Singapore, the United Kingdom, Australia, Mexico, Brazil, and Japan. Locate your local office at: **international.cengage.com/region**

Cengage Learning products are represented in Canada by Nelson Education, Ltd.

For your course and learning solutions, visit **academic.cengage.com**

Purchase any of our products at your local college store or at our preferred online store **www.ichapters.com**

Printed in Canada
1 2 3 4 5 6 7 11 10 09 08 07

To my wonderful family:
Jarrod, Garett, Jenna, and Jayden.
And to Jim and Ron for their ongoing support.

AUTHOR BIOGRAPHIES

James S. O'Rourke teaches management and corporate communication at the University of Notre Dame, where he is the Arthur F. and Mary J. O'Neil Director of the Fanning Center for Business Communication and Concurrent Professor of Management. In a career spanning four decades, he has earned an international reputation in business and corporate communication. BUSINESS WEEK magazine has repeatedly named him one of the "outstanding faculty" in Notre Dame's Mendoza College of business. His publications include MANAGEMENT COMMUNICATION: A CASE-ANALYSIS APPROACH from Prentice-Hall, now in third edition, and BUSINESS COMMUNICATION: A FRAMEWORK FOR SUCCESS from Thomson Learning. O'Rourke is also senior editor of a seven-book series on Managerial Communication and is principal author or directing editor of more than 150 management and corporate communication case studies. O'Rourke is a graduate of Notre Dame with advanced degrees from Temple University, the University of New Mexico, and a Ph.D. in Communication from the S. I. Newhouse School of Syracuse University. He has held faculty appointments at the United States Air Force Academy, the Defense Information School, the United States Air War College, and the Communications Institute of Ireland. He was a Gannett Foundation Teaching Fellow at Indiana University in the 1980s, and a graduate student in language and history at Christ's College, Cambridge University, in England during the 1970s. O'Rourke is a member and trustee of The Arthur W. Page Society and the Institute for Public Relations; he is a member of the Reputation Institute, and the Management Communication Association. He is also a regular consultant to Fortune 500 and mid-size businesses throughout North America.

Sandra Dean Collins currently teaches management communication for the Mendoza College of Business at the University of Notre Dame. Her courses include business writing, business speaking, conflict management, persuasion, and negotiation. She has also taught statistics and research methods for the university. She conducts team training for the Mendoza College of Business and local organizations and consults with small and mid-sized organizations on communication and team related issues. Her background includes a Ph.D. is Social Psychology and experience in sales, purchasing, and banking.

Editor: James S. O'Rourke
Affiliation: University of Notre Dame

TABLE OF CONTENTS

CHAPTER THREE: True Persuasion: Changing Minds 33

CHAPTER FOUR: The Emotional Side of Persuasion 53

FOREWORD

In recent years, for a variety of reasons, communication has grown increasingly complex. The issues that seemed so straightforward, so simple not long ago are now somehow different, more complicated. Has the process changed? Have the elements of communication or the barriers to success been altered? What's different now? Why has this all gotten more difficult?

Several issues are at work here, not the least of which is pacing. Information, images, events, and human activity all move at a much faster pace than they did just a decade ago. Among the more popular, hip new business magazines in recent years is *Fast Company*. Readers are reminded that it's not just a matter of tempo, but a new way of living we're experiencing.

Technology has changed things, as well. We're now able to communicate with almost anyone, almost anywhere, 24/7 with very little effort and very little professional assistance. It's all possible because of cellular telephone technology, digital imaging, the Internet, fiber optics, global positioning satellites, teleconferencing codecs, high-speed data processing, online data storage and ... well, the list goes on and on. What's new this morning will be old hat by lunch.

Culture has intervened in our lives in some important ways. Very few parts of the world are inaccessible any more. Other people's beliefs, practices, perspectives, and possessions are as familiar to us as our own. And for many of us, we're only now coming to grips with the idea that our own beliefs aren't shared by everyone and that culture is hardly value-neutral.

The nature of the world in which we live—one that's wired, connected, mobile, fast-paced, iconically visual, and far less driven by logic—has changed in some not-so-subtle ways in recent days. The organizations that employ us and the businesses that depend on our skills now recognize that communication is at the center of what it means to be successful. And at the heart of what it means to be human.

To operate profitably means that business must now conduct itself in responsible ways, keenly attuned to the needs and interests of its stakeholders. And, more than ever, the communication skills and capabilities we bring to the workplace are essential to our success, both at the individual and at the societal level.

So, what does that mean to you as a prospective manager or executive-in-training? For one thing, it means that communication will involve more than simple writing, speaking, and listening skills. It will involve new contexts, new applications, and new technologies. Much of what will affect the balance of your lives has yet to be invented. But when it is, you'll have to learn to live with it and make it work on your behalf.

The book you've just opened is volume seven in a series that will help you to do all of those things and more. It's direct, simple, and very compact. Professor Sandra Collins of Notre Dame explores the processes at work in *Persuasion*. Her approach is at once theoretical and practical, as she takes you through the latest research findings in behavioral psychology and then shows how they can be applied in workplace settings ranging from corporate offices to sales conferences. Numerous examples and illustrations will help you understand why each of us comes to believe what we do, and how we're each susceptible to influence from others around us. It's a fascinating read and a pragmatic application of both scientific principles and professional best practices.

The first volume in our series of seven comes from my colleague Professor Bonnie Yarbrough of the University of North Carolina Greensboro. Her aim is not to provide you with a broad-based education in either business or communication, but rather to pinpoint the issues and ideas most closely associated with *Leading Groups and Teams*. Her approach draws on both time-honored principles as well as the latest research in group dynamics and demonstrates why team communication may be among the more important yet least understood communication issues for managers.

In this series' second volume, Professors Sedlack of Notre Dame, Barbara Shwom of Northwestern University, and Chicago management consultant Karl Keller focus on *Graphics and Visual Communication for Managers*. They'll show you subtle differences in typeface, font size, page layout, and document design, as well as help you develop skills in color appreciation, screening, cropping, graph design, and the effective use of PowerPoint to make you more capable as a business communicator.

Professor Sandra Collins, the author of two other books in the series, is a social psychologist by training. The conceptual framework she offers in *Managing Conflict and Workplace Relationships* involves far more than dispute resolution or determining how limited resources can be allocated equitably among people who think they all deserve more. She shows us how to manage our own emotions, as well as those of others. Creative conflict, organizational harmony, and synchronicity in the workplace are issues that too many of us have avoided simply because we didn't understand them or didn't know what to say.

In volume four, Professor Elizabeth Tuleja of the Wharton School at the University of Pennsylvania and the Chinese University of Hong Kong, examines *Intercultural Communication for Business*, looking both broadly and specifically at issues and opportunities that will seem increasingly important as the business world shrinks and grows more interdependent. As time zones blur and fewer restrictions are imposed on the global movement of capital, raw materials, finished goods, and human labor, people will cling fiercely to the ways in which they were enculturated as youngsters. Culture will become a defining characteristic, not only of peoples and nations, but of organizations and industries.

Volume five, again by Professor Sandra Collins, explores issues associated with *Interpersonal Communication: Listening and Responding*. Her work draws on the latest findings in behavioral psychology and demonstrates why listening and personal interaction may be among the most important yet underdeveloped skills we possess. Becoming an active interpersonal communicator, tuning in to the emotional as well as cognitive content of what we hear, and learning to provide timely, targeted, and meaningful responses are among the most important things we can do for our customers, employees, co-workers, shareholders, and others we deal with in the workplace each day.

In volume six, Professor Carolyn Boulger Karlson of Notre Dame explores the process of communication and entrepreneurship in *Writing and Presenting a Business Plan*. In a step-by-step approach, she takes us from good ideas ("remember, an idea is not a business, it's just an idea") through feasibility analysis, to a fully developed business plan. She explains how to identify and influence sources of funding for a new venture, how to package your ideas for the marketplace, and how to present your plan to a venture capitalist. Detailed formats and complete business plans are included.

This is an interesting, exciting, and highly practical series of books. They're small, of course, not intended as comprehensive texts, but as supplemental readings, or as stand-alone volumes for modular courses or seminars. They're engaging because they've been written by people who are smart, passionate about what they do, and more than happy to share what they know. And I've been happy to edit the series, first, because these authors are all friends and colleagues whom I know and have come to trust. Secondly, I've enjoyed the task because this is really interesting stuff. Read on. There is a lot to learn here, new horizons to explore, and new ways to think about human communication.

James S. O'Rourke, IV
The Eugene D. Fanning Center
Mendoza College of Business
University of Notre Dame
Notre Dame, Indiana

MANAGERIAL COMMUNICATION SERIES
Series Editor: James O'Rourke, IV

The Managerial Communication Series includes 7 Modules covering Leadership, Graphics and Visual Communication, Conflict Management, Intercultural Communication, Interpersonal Communication, Writing and Preparing a Business Plan, and Persuasion. Each module can be used alone or customized with any of our best-selling Business Communication textbooks. You may also combine these modules with others in the series to create a course-specific Managerial Communication text.

MODULE 1: LEADING GROUPS AND TEAMS

ISBN-10: 0-324-58417-2
ISBN-13: 978-0-324-58417-2

Module 1 addresses one of the most important functions a manager performs: putting together effective teams and creating the conditions for their success. This edition describes the major theories of group formation and group functioning, and explains how to create, lead, and manage teams.

MODULE 2: GRAPHICS AND VISUAL COMMUNICATION FOR MANAGERS

ISBN-10: 0-324-58418-0
ISBN-13: 978-0-324-58418-9

Module 2 explains the details involved in crafting graphic images that tell a story clearly, crisply, and with powerful visual impact. Using a step-by-step approach, it demonstrates how to create PowerPoint® files that support and enhance a presentation without dominating or overpowering the content of a talk.

MODULE 3: MANAGING CONFLICT AND WORKPLACE RELATIONSHIPS

ISBN-10: 0-324-58419-9
ISBN-13: 978-0-324-58419-6

Module 3 uses an approach that involves far more than dispute resolution or figuring out how limited resources can be distributed equitably among people who think they all deserve more. Readers will learn how to manage their own emotions, as well as those of others in the workplace.

MODULE 6:
WRITING AND PRESENTING A BUSINESS PLAN

ISBN-10: 0-324-58422-9
ISBN-13: 978-0-324-58422-6

Module 6 reviews the entire process of writing and presenting a business plan. From idea generation to feasibility analysis, and from writing the plan to presenting it to various audience groups, this text covers all the steps necessary to develop and start a business.

MODULE 7:
PERSUASION

ISBN-10: 0-324-58421-0
ISBN-13: 978-0-324-58421-9

Module 7 provides a brief overview of both classic and recent social science research in the area of social influence. It offers applications for the business leader for shaping organizational culture, motivating employees, and being an influential manager.

MODULE 4:
INTERCULTURAL COMMUNICATION FOR BUSINESS

ISBN-10: 0-324-58420-2
ISBN-13: 978-0-324-58420-2

Module 4 examines Intercultural Communication for Business, looking both broadly and specifically at issues and opportunities that will seem increasingly important as the business world grows more interdependent.

MODULE 5:
INTERPERSONAL COMMUNICATION: LISTENING AND RESPONDING

ISBN-10: 0-324-58416-4
ISBN-13: 978-0-324-58416-5

Module 5 explores how successful companies and effective managers use listening as a strategic communication tool at all levels of the organization. Common barriers to listening — including culture, perceptions, and personal agendas — are discussed, and strategies for overcoming them are offered.

INTRODUCTION

"Influential person" might not be part of your job title, and it won't be stamped on your birth certificate—but it could be, because that's when your influence over others begins. From your first cry, you are influencing others. We are all agents of change. We are all influencers. Whether you are selling the merits of your idea to your team, informing a customer of the benefits of your product, convincing your spouse that a vacation in Maui actually could be a matter of life and death, or getting your child to eat his peas, you are using your powers of social influence to create change in the attitudes, beliefs, or behaviors of others. The question isn't whether or not you will try to influence others, but rather, how effective will you be. Are you getting the kind of change you seek?

I became interested in the topic of persuasion while I was a student of social psychology studying research papers about attitude change. After a lifetime of influencing other people through smiling and asking nicely, arguing semi-effectively, or just being annoying to the point they couldn't take it anymore and gave in, I was fascinated to learn that scientific research had been done in the area of persuasion and social influence. I believed that if I studied that research thoroughly, it might impart something to me that would make me more influential.

The more studying I did, however, the more I discovered that I did not know and, in fact, the more I learned that no one really knows. Social influence is a little bit science, a little bit art, and a little bit mystery. Some people are just going to be better at it than others and sometimes even the very best won't be able to create a desired change. But these challenges—basically the challenges of working with people and trying to understand them—are what make the subject matter so interesting.

In this text, you will learn some techniques that, if applied correctly, will indeed make you more effective at influencing others. Importantly, you will also learn how to recognize techniques that are being used in an attempt to influence you. We will take two, often separate approaches to this topic. We'll explore both social psychological theories of persuasion and social influence and also look at argumentation and evidence.

In Chapter 1, we talk about persuasion and distinguish it from other forms of social influence. We also talk about the ethical questions that surround topics of social influence. A student in one of my classes asked, "How can you influence others without manipulating them and isn't manipulating other people unethical?" It's a good question and one that ought to be asked perhaps more often than it is. We'll learn about a framework to help us make judgments about whether a message meant to persuade is ethical.

Not all social influence occurs as a result of carefully constructed arguments. In fact, a great deal of social influence isn't even intentional. In Chapter 2, we discuss forms of social influence, such as compliance, conformity, and obedience that surround us, affect us, and that we use frequently, but that often fall short of what we will call true persuasion.

In Chapter 3, we look at building a solid argument and using quality evidence to support our positions. We explore the research on attitudes and attitude change. We also consider propaganda and manipulated arguments that might appear sound at first glance, but that fail to stand up to careful scrutiny.

Many people believe they are rational decision-makers and they may be to a large degree. However, we would be unwise to overlook the power of emotions to influence others. In Chapter 4, we consider the emotional side of messages and the effectiveness of various types of appeals that seek to arouse a specific emotional response, such as fear.

In both your personal and your professional life, you are influential. This book has the modest aim of sharing research findings that you can apply to help you become more effective in your efforts to ethically influence others.

Sandra Dean Collins
Notre Dame, Indiana
January 2008

1 PERSUASION: WHAT SHOULD YOU KNOW AND WHY?

What is persuasion? How much should you know about it? Let's start with the second question first. Consider this story from a woman sitting in her home in the middle of the day, minding her own business:

This woman was working on a project when the doorbell rang. At the door was a handsome young man, casually dressed and holding a clipboard. He introduced himself and said that he was with a certain trash removal company and he noticed that she wasn't one of their customers. He indicated that a neighbor across the street (referring to the neighbor by name) suggested he come over. He then mentioned a few of her other neighbors who use his company's service.

It felt very chummy, but she wasn't ready to fall for it. Before he could finish, she interrupted him and told him that she didn't want to switch from her current service. She was very clear in saying she didn't want to switch. He was accepting of that but didn't leave. Instead, he politely asked why she didn't want to switch. Her explanation was that her current company had given her great service, even hauling away, with no complaints, the pieces of a privacy fence she had taken down. He said he could appreciate that and explained that he was familiar with the company but knew that his company provided service that was just as good. He added that his company was a local, family-owned business and her company wasn't. He pointed out his customers were putting money back into the community. He almost convinced her with that because it sounded like the "right" thing to do, as if choosing a trash service were a judgment about values. Instead, she countered with a values argument of her own and told him she believed in repaying good service with continued patronage.

He again agreed and said he thought that was right unless there was a good reason to change. Then he mentioned that he was able to save some of her neighbors, who had previously used the company she was with, about 25% on their trash collection bill for precisely the same level of service. Her resolve was weakening, but she still said, no. He responded by asking if she would be willing to pay *more* for the same level of service and lose the added benefit of a locally-owned company. He just wanted to confirm that was her position. She had always thought of herself as very frugal, always negotiating the best deal, never overpaying, so when he put it like that, she just couldn't say no anymore even though she really didn't want to switch.

What does this story tell us about reasons for studying persuasion? First, getting people to change their minds and their behaviors can be difficult. When we talk about persuasion, we are referring to creating some kind of change, and people generally don't like to change, especially if it is someone else's idea. Second, different people respond to different appeals. If the young man in the story had used just one appeal, he probably wouldn't have been successful. He had to try different messages until he produced one that was motivating for this particular person. But perhaps the most practical and important reasons for understanding persuasion are the final two illustrated by the story: We are all users of persuasion and we are all consumers of persuasion.

In our personal and professional lives, no matter what our industry or role, we will attempt to influence others, probably many times, each day. From the time you get up in the morning, attempting to persuade your kids to hurry and get ready for school, to the meeting where convincing your boss you should take the lead on the next project, to convincing your client that pink really is the new black, or persuading your spouse to watch Leno instead of Letterman, you are an agent of influence every day. In fact, even when we are simply making a statement, to the extent that we hope to be believed by our audience, we are attempting to persuade. If we do spend so much of our time in any typical day attempting to influence others, it makes sense to understand how persuasion works and how we can do it as well as we can.

MESSAGES IN OUR LIVES

We are bombarded with persuasive messages all the time. Observe the room where you are right now and spot any messages meant to influence you. Are you able to see any product labels or packaging? Do your clothes or shoes feature a brand name or logo? Is there a radio or T.V. playing anywhere in the background? If you are alone with this book in an isolation chamber, then look at the cover of the book and the inside pages that offer information about other titles in this series. If you are conscious, you have little hope of escaping messages meant to influence you.

So what messages should we be influenced by? That's the principal reason for studying persuasion. We are consumers of persuasive messages. We have no choice. But we can choose to be wise consumers of persuasive messages. We can learn about how to critically analyze messages meant to influence us in order to improve our decision making. In the story above, our young homeowner was influenced by something we'll learn about later called cognitive dissonance. Perhaps the decision to switch service providers was a good one, perhaps not. Time will tell, but as the one making the decision, the homeowner might have been able to make a better decision by understanding what was going on.

In our effort to answer the question, "Why understand persuasion?" we've used the terms "persuasion" and "influence" almost interchangeably. But is all social influence persuasion? This brings us back to the other question we were going to answer: What is persuasion? It turns out, that's not such an easy question to answer.

Robert Gass and John Seiter, in their book *Persuasion, Social Influence, and Compliance Gaining*, identify several issues involved in defining persuasion in general and ways of distinguishing it from other forms of social influence. Those issues include effectiveness, intention, internalized change, and perception of choice.[1] We'll explore each one and then show how we will settle these definitional issues for the purposes of this book. Let's begin our exploration with John's story, which illustrates several of these definitional issues.

JOHN'S STORY

This was going to be an exciting day for John and his business partner Dale. They owned Crooked Zen, a small beverage company specializing in designer energy drinks and specialty teas. They were ready to expand into a new market: Chilled coffee drinks made with African coffee beans from Kenya and Ethiopia. Today, John was meeting with a representative from a bottling company he hoped to work with and needed to convince the representative that Crooked Zen was worth very favorable terms. Dale had been called out of town to meet with a major account who frequently demanded personal visits, so John was on his own.

John felt eager and optimistic about the meeting. He had joked with his assistant that he was wearing his "credibility blue" suit and a "conservative, yet dynamic" striped tie. He had even gone for a jog that morning to invigorate his mind work. Of course, he had needed 15 minutes of convincing himself to get up, as he lay in bed repeatedly hitting the snooze button.

The idea to expand into chilled coffee products had occurred by chance. Dale and John had agreed that it was time for the company to expand and were looking for ideas when John happened to overhear a woman in line at the grocery store. The woman was discussing an article she had read about the economic problems facing Kenyan coffee farmers. She argued how she would happily pay more for a cup of coffee if she thought if would benefit those farmers. The wheels of John's mind immediately started cranking out an entire line of coffee products and a marketing plan that would appeal to a target market filled with people just like this woman.

John had shared the idea with Dale, who was very enthusiastic. He then worked feverishly developing the idea and presented it to the staff at an all-hands meeting the next day. They all nodded in eager agreement, but John had the sense they were not all completely convinced this was a wise move. Now, two months later, as John prepared to leave for his meeting, everyone at Crooked Zen acted as if they were completely on board, even if not thoroughly convinced.

DEFINING PERSUASION

In John's brief story we see several examples of influence at work. The most obvious is the planned meeting between John and the representative from the bottling company in which John hopes to make a case for Crooked Zen receiving favorable terms for bottling their drinks. Most people would agree that when John finally makes his argument to the representative, that will be an attempt at persuasion.

But what if he fails? What if John makes his best case, and the bottling representative says, "no?" Is this still persuasion if it's ineffective? Does a message need to be effective in order to be considered persuasive? Some would argue "yes," while others would argue "no." It doesn't help matters that effectiveness itself is difficult to define and sometimes hard to determine.

- Is a message effective if some of the audience is persuaded and some is not? John gave his pitch to his entire staff and some were persuaded to buy into the idea and others were not.
- Is a message effective if it does not result in the specific change the persuader was seeking, but change in the desired direction still occurs? Perhaps the representative from the bottling company wouldn't agree to John's request at this time, but his attitude about the project is very favorable.
- Is a message effective if it doesn't produce the desired result by itself, but contributes to the desired result when combined with other messages? John's employees, who remained skeptical after his initial pitch, are likely to receive many more messages about the coffee venture and the cumulative effect of those messages might be the buy-in John is looking for.

Another difficulty in defining persuasion is intent. If communication that influences another person was unintentional, is it still persuasion? Communication can be unintentional in two ways: Unintended audiences and unintended outcomes.

- **Unintended audiences.** When John was in the grocery story listening to the woman in line, she had a profound influence on him. But she certainly didn't mean to influence John; she probably didn't intend for him to hear what she was saying.
- **Unintended consequences.** The woman in our story wasn't trying to persuade John, but she was probably trying to be persuasive. She was probably trying to persuade her listener of the seriousness of the economic problems for Kenyan coffee farmers and perhaps even the wisdom of a company exercising and advertising fair trade with this group. A better example of unintended consequences would be a new employee observing the typical behaviors of other employees and adopting them in order to fit in with the group. For example, let's say employees in a particular department talk about a weekly television show that they all watch. A new employee might start watching that show to be able to join in the conversation. The group's influence on the new employee wasn't intentional; it was just a by-product of their conversation.

Whether the change resulting from a message must be internalized in order to be considered persuasion, or if an outward change that is not internalized is good enough are other issues in persuasion.

In our story, John created internalized change in some of his staff. They bought into his idea and truly believed in it. For some other employees, however, the change was never internalized. They changed outwardly. They acted supportive and went through all the right motions, but they didn't really buy into the message.

Another issue in defining persuasion is the requirement for more than one person. In our story, John spends some time convincing himself to get out of bed in the morning to go jogging. Is he persuading himself? Some definitions of persuasion require at least two people to be involved in the process, while other definitions allow for self-persuasion. Some researchers believe that all persuasion is self-persuasion, arguing that it is what *we think* about the message we receive from another source that persuades us, not the message itself. Therefore, our thoughts are persuading us and that could be regarded as self-persuasion.

The issue of freedom of choice is a point of disagreement in the definition of persuasion, as well. In our story, John's business partner Dale is unable to attend the meeting with the bottling company representative because he's been called out of town by an account who frequently demands personal visits. Did the customer persuade Dale to come visit? If Dale thought he might lose the account if he didn't go, he may have felt that he had little choice. Some students argue that there's always a choice. Even if your boss tells you to do something—or you'll be fired, you could choose to be fired, and that is certainly true. However, does that represent persuasion or is it something else?

Another point to make about defining persuasion, but one over which there is little if any debate, is the that persuasion is not necessarily verbal. John wears a suit and tie he thinks will help him be more effective. Even though he's not relying exclusively on his clothes to seal the deal, his appearance could contribute to his success.

For the purposes of this book, we will draw a distinction between other forms of social influence and what we'll call true persuasion. *True* persuasion will be limited to an intentional, internalized change in attitude, belief, or behavior brought about by communication, where some degree of freedom of choice is perceived by the recipient. Even though we allow for the possibility that true persuasion occurs as a result of a person's reaction to the message, meaning self-persuasion, for the purposes of this book, we will focus on the transfer of meaning between communicators.

This leaves *unintended* influence, situations in which there appears to be no choice; this amounts to change which is not internalized under the heading of other forms of influence. Other forms of influence that don't meet this narrow definition include conformity, compliance, and obedience. This is not to say these forms of influence aren't important. Far from it. These other forms of social influence are pervasive. We are exposed to them constantly, influenced by them immeasurably, and employ them regularly. So, in this book we will look at all these various forms of social influence.

THE BASIC CONSIDERATIONS FOR SOCIAL INFLUENCE

No matter what sort of social influence you are experiencing as an influencer or recipient, some basic facts hold true. From the perspective of the persuader, the effectiveness of all efforts at social influence can be improved by considering four principles and their relationship to one another. These principles all affect the audience you are hoping to persuade. Note that throughout this book when we refer to "audience" that can be just one person or many.

1. **Know what you want from your audience.** Be very clear about what you expect from them. Know your objective and recognize that a range of responses is possible from your audience. If you don't know what you want, how do you expect to get it?

2. **Know your credibility with your audience.** What do they know about your experience and expertise? Do you have a proven track record with them? Do they see you as similar to them in

terms of goals, processes, etc? What's the political landscape and where do you fit in? What's the power distribution between you and your audience?

3. **Motivate your audience to make the change you're seeking.** You absolutely must know what is important to your audience and what will motivate them to make the change you're seeking. Motivating them to meet your objective doesn't always require you to gain buy-in from your audience. You don't always need them to share your vision, buy the T-shirt, and put the bumper sticker on their car. It just means they will do what you want. So, if you tell your production crew they need to produce twenty units by the end of the day or they'll all be working on the weekend, and they produce twenty units, you've managed to motivate your crew. You didn't have to tell them about the contract you stand to lose if you don't meet the production goals; you didn't have to get them to see you as a great leader and a visionary. In this case, you didn't need to. Now if you have a consistent problem meeting production goals, perhaps you do need to step up your leadership, change attitudes and improve morale. But that's a different goal. The point here is this: You must know what motivates your audience to meet the specific objective you have for a particular message. A strong argument with lots of supporting evidence may not be very interesting or motivating to some audiences, despite its debate-star quality.

4. **Make it easy for them to do what you ask.** Remove the barriers that prevent your audience from doing what you want. Barriers can take many forms. One might be the extra effort the audience is required to exert because you didn't provide them with something they needed in order to do what you asked, such as a response card, a stamped and addressed envelope, or an address, Web site, or phone number that they'll have to look up. A barrier can be the counterargument they are thinking about while you are making your case and that you fail to refute. A barrier might be the foundational information you didn't provide before you started your argument. Barriers you can't do much about, such as a lack of funding, authority, or resources, are indications that you have the wrong audience. Make sure your audience can do what you're asking and then make it as easy as you possibly can.

Don't be misled into thinking you can't expect your audience to do difficult things. The relationship among the four principles must be taken into account. People can be persuaded to engage in the most difficult of challenges if they are motivated enough. Dr. Martin Luther King, Jr. created a passionate desire for change that motivated people to behave in ways that were not easy, but he made it as easy for his audience as he could through his credibility, his example, and the fervor stirred by his words.

THE ASSUMPTIONS MADE FOR THIS BOOK

An assumption made in writing this book was that the reader is most likely a business professional or business student, busy, concerned with gaining tools that can be immediately applied in the workplace, and not terribly interested in research. The approach of this book is to provide a summary and practical application for the profusion of academic literature on persuasion.

That said, this book does explain some of the classic research in the area of social influence and persuasion. This is done for two reasons. First, some classic studies are well known in general and familiar to the business student who has had a class in management or organizational behavior. It's necessary to mention these classic, seminal studies in order to give the reader some foundational knowledge of the subject.

The second reason for including some exploration of research is to abide by one of the major goals of this book, which is to make the reader a more critical consumer of persuasive messages. Claims that are incorporated into your body of knowledge and used in your decision making should be analyzed and evaluated. Far too often, advice for business professionals is based on little more than one person's opinion and limited experience. You should question how claims and suggestions were derived and what gives them credibility—that is true for the claims made in this book as well. Critical consumers of persuasion need to know where recommendations are coming from. Something needs to back them up: Experience, expertise, or scientific research.

Research that looks at human behavior produces findings in the form of probabilities, not absolutes. Social scientists seek to understand general tendencies in human behavior. Even those who study individual differences, such as personality characteristics, attempt to understand how those differences generally affect behavior. Thus, the research findings from social scientific endeavors give us ideas about how people *in general* might *typically* behave or respond. What no social science can do is accurately predict how any single individual will behave in a given situation. Furthermore, no researcher of persuasion can tell you how to construct a persuasive message that will be 100% effective with your entire audience or be guaranteed to get the desired response from a given individual.

For a variety of reasons, you may not get the exact response you expect, based on previous research findings, from a given member of your audience. Take, for example, a message from human resources at your company encouraging employees to take advantage of an offer to pay for gym memberships at a gym of the employees' choice. The human resources manager may use every piece of science available to construct her message and may still have a small response to the offer. Perhaps some employees already have gym memberships, some don't work out and would prefer to never work out, some don't have the time, and some are insulted by the company's attempt to intrude upon their personal lives and suggest they need to work out. Other employees will respond favorably to the message and will get the gym membership.

So, you might ask, what is the point of discussing applications of the social science if it doesn't work? Nothing works with everyone all the time. The goal of the information presented in this book is to increase your likelihood of achieving your goals of social influence to the highest likelihood possible. Using the science available won't give the HR manager a message that is 100% effective, but it is likely to give her a message that is significantly more effective. As Joe Gideon says to Victoria in the classic film, *All that Jazz*, "I can't make you a great dancer . . . but I can make you a better dancer."[2] Our hope for this book is to make you a better persuader.

A second assumption made for this book is that we are interested in being ethical agents of influence. Over the last several years, ethics has become center of conversations in business schools and organizations, as well it should judging from the continuing barrage of headlines revealing unethical and illegal behavior in the business world. A 2005–2006 integrity survey at the accounting firm KPMG indicated that 74% of employees nationally had observed misconduct that would have a serious, negative impact on public trust[3]—a number that remained virtually unchanged since 2000, despite Enron, WorldCom, and other public scandals.

Questions of ethics are perhaps more important in the area of social influence than anywhere else, particularly for people in positions of power. Is it always right to influence others if we know we can? May we use any tactics we believe will work? What responsibility does the agent of influence have for negative consequences that result? Perhaps the most important question but not the easiest to answer is, how does an agent of influence judge the ethics of a message meant to influence?

Traditional means of discussing ethics are of some, but limited, use. The customary frameworks for ethics offer various approaches that for our purposes can be captured essentially by one question that taps into their core, that we can ask ourselves when we are deciding to prepare or deliver a persuasive message:

- **The Utilitarian Approach.** Does this action provide the most good and cause the least harm of all available alternatives?
- **The Rights Approach.** Does this action protect and respect human dignity, treating people as ends in themselves, not as means?
- **The Fairness or Justice Approach.** Does this action treat all equals equally?

- **The Common Good Approach.** Does this action consider what is best for all others in community?
- **The Virtue Approach.** Does this action reflect a virtue that is consistent with ideal virtues?

These are helpful, general approaches to evaluating ethics, but another methods specific to the evaluation of persuasive communication is perhaps more useful. The TARES test was developed by Sherry Baker and David Martinson as a test for "persuasion professionals" to evaluate the ethics of persuasive messages. Persuasion professionals, according to the authors, are people who work in the areas of advertising and public relations. They suggest that persuasive messages should serve some "moral last end" such as increased information and maximized choice, rather than an immediate, instrumental end, such as increased sales. The authors set about to produce a set of principles to set ethical boundaries for persuasive communicators. The TARES test consists of five principles: Truthfulness, authenticity of the persuader, respect for the recipient, equity of the persuasive appeal, and social responsibility.[4]

TRUTHFULNESS OF THE MESSAGE

Deceit is considered to be an assault of sorts on the receivers of an untrue message that takes away their power and control. People are harmed by deception because they depend on information to make choices, and their ability to make informed choices is stripped away when deceived. Questions persuaders can ask themselves to test the truthfulness of their message include:

- Does this message lead others to believe what I, myself, do not believe?
- Would I feel this message was non-deceptive if communicated to me?
- Is this message substantially complete?
- Has this appeal downplayed relevant evidence?
- Will people have reason to question my honesty as a result of this message?

AUTHENTICITY OF THE PERSUADER

The authors of the TARES test use the term authenticity to describe a person's genuineness and ability to act in harmony with one's true self. It is a combination of personal virtue, sincerity, loyalty to one's highest self in a world where many roles we must occupy will have conflicting goals. Questions persuaders can ask to determine if their message is authentic include:

- Does this action compromise my integrity?
- Although I may have the right to do this, is this the right thing to do?
- Do a personally believe in this product, service, event, etc.?
- Would I openly and publicly advocate for this cause?
- Would I advocate this product or service to people I love?

RESPECT FOR THE RECIPIENT

Like the traditional Rights approach to ethics, the TARES test ensures that people are treated as end in themselves, rather than means to some other goal. Respect for the recipient is the core of the TARES test and motivates its other principles. Respect for others, according to the TARES test, includes appealing to the best, rather than the worst, in the persuadee. Appealing to baser instincts, without regard for the consequences to the persuadee would not be respectful. For example, the Ashley Madison Agency, whose tag line is "When monogamy becomes monotony" is a dating service that connects married individuals interested in having extramarital relationships. A southern California billboard of theirs which read, "Life is short, have an affair." would be unlikely to pass the TARES test for respect.[5] Questions to determine if a persuasive communication meets the test of respect for the recipient include:

- Have I respected the receivers of this message by appealing to their higher inclinations and by not exploiting their lower, baser inclinations?
- Does the message facilitate recipients' capacity to reflect and to make responsible choices about their lives?

- Have I taken the rights, interests, and well-being of others into consideration as much as my own?
- Does the action promote raw self-interest at the unfair expense of or to the detriment of recipients?

EQUITY OF THE PERSUASIVE APPEAL

Vulnerable audiences should not be targeted unfairly. Claims should not be created that are beyond the recipient's ability to understand, for the purposes of exploiting them. For example, the poor and illiterate should not be unfairly targeted with invitations to participate in paid drug trials that involve complicated descriptions of the risks involved. Questions to help determine the equity of an appeal include:

- Is the power of persuasion used fairly and justly?
- Would I feel that the persuasion in this situation was fair, just, and ethical if it were communicated to me or people I know?
- Have I unfairly targeted vulnerable audiences?
- Do the receivers of the message fully understand the costs and potential harms to themselves and others of what I am advocating?

SOCIAL RESPONSIBILITY

Social responsibility requires consideration of the effects of persuasive communication on the community and society as a whole. Messages shouldn't serve to meet the narrow goals of an organization at cost to the greater common good. Questions to determine the social responsibility of a message include:

- Will the product or issue I am promoting cause harm to individuals or to society?
- Does this action recognize the interdependency of persons in society?
- Does this message strain understanding and cooperation among constituent groups of society?
- Have I unfairly stereotyped constituent groups of society in the communication?

DISCUSSION QUESTIONS

1. Why is it important for managers to make the distinction between true persuasion and other sorts of social influence?

2. As the executive director of a not-for-profit organization, you have been having trouble recruiting board members. You currently have fewer board members than is required by your by-laws and you are getting desperate. You arrange to meet with a retired executive who just moved into the community. At a lunch meeting you explain to her that serving on the board is easy: There are only four meetings a year, no preparation is required, and it will be a great opportunity to rub elbows with the movers and shakers of the community. Are there any ethical concerns with this situation?

3. An energy drink was introduced called Cocaine. On the packaging the product name appeared to be spelled out in a white granular substance that resembles cocaine powder. The following messages were part of the marketing campaign for the beverage. Analyze the messages using the TARES test.

   - "The Legal Alternative"
   - "Speed in a Can"
   - "Liquid Cocaine"
   - "Cocaine-Instant Rush"

- "The question you have to ask yourself is: Can I handle the rush?"
- "This beverage should be consumed by responsible adults. Failure to adhere to this warning may result in excess excitement, stamina, . . . and possible feeling of euphoria"
- Contains: "Inositol . . . reduces cholesterol in the blood; it helps prevent hardening of the arteries, and may protect nerve fibers from excess glucose damage. Inositol has a natural calming effect and may be used in the treatment of anxiety, depression, and obsessive-compulsive disorder without the side effects of prescription medications."

ENDNOTES

1. R. H. Gass and J. S. Seiter, *Persuasion, Social Influence, and Compliance Gaining,* 3rd ed. (Boston: Pearson Education, Inc., 2007): 21–41.
2. R. A. Aurthur and B. Fosse. *All that Jazz.* Released 20 December 1979 by Columbia Pictures Corporation.
3. *KPMG Forensic Integrity Survey 2005–2006.* Retrieved 11/6/07 from http://www.globalcompliance.com/pdf/KPMG%20Integrity%20Survey%2005.pdf.
4. S. Baker and D. L. Martinson, "The TARES Test: Five Principles for Ethical Persuasion," *Journal of Mass Media Ethics* 16, no. 2 & 3 (2001): 148–175.
5. L. Miller, "Agency Makes no Apology," September 27, 2007, KABC-TV/DT, Retrieved from http://abclocal.go.com/kabc/story?section=local&id=5679613.

2 SOCIAL INFLUENCE WITHOUT TRUE PERSUASION: CONFORMITY, COMPLIANCE, AND OBEDIENCE

When we want to influence others we are seeking to create change in them, either in their attitudes, beliefs, behaviors, perhaps even their values, or some combination of these. To get the change we are seeking, we may need to deliver multiple messages consisting of carefully crafted arguments and expose our credentials to build our credibility. On the other hand, we may not. To get the change we're seeking, we might simply need to ask nicely, or threaten soberly, or just be in a group that people want to be part of. Forms of social influence that fall short of the definition of true persuasion we chiseled out in Chapter 1 include conformity, compliance, and obedience.

Conformity fails to meet our definition of true persuasion because it often lacks intent. People are motivated to conform to groups and, therefore, groups don't have to work hard to persuade people to conform. Another way in which conformity is unlike persuasion, at least sometimes, is that change is not internalized. Sometimes people conform outwardly to the expectations of the group, without conforming inwardly.

The lack of internalization is the distinction between compliance and true persuasion. Compliance is the response to a direct request. If your colleague asks you for a ride to the airport on Friday night and you agree, you've complied. Compliance doesn't mean internal agreement. You may have other things you would rather do on a Friday night and not be happy about driving to the airport, but your colleague has secured your compliance even without your ingratiation.

If you feel like you could have told your colleague "no," but instead said "yes," you've complied. If you feel like you really didn't have any choice, then you've obeyed. Let's say it's your boss who needs the ride, and you don't feel like you've been asked to provide the ride so much as told that you will provide the ride. The perception of little freedom of choice and lack of internalization differentiates obedience from true persuasion.

In this chapter, we'll discuss each of these forms of social influence, some of the classic research in each area, and some practical application for managers.

CONFORMITY

Do you think of yourself as a nonconformist? When students are asked this question in class, many of them will raise their hand or nod in agreement. In Western society, where cultural values emphasize independence, it is not surprising that many of us like to think of ourselves as being nonconformists to some degree. But most of us, when we really give it some consideration, don't believe we are truly nonconformist. Even the students, who conform to the rules of the classroom by raising their hands in response to the question and by nodding their Nike ball cap covered heads "yes" almost in unison, will admit, reluctantly as they cross their arms over their Abercrombie and Fitch t-shirts, that they are not really nonconformists. We hesitate to admit being conformists because of the relatively negative connotation associated with being a conformist in a culture that values independence so highly.

Relax. It's okay to be a conformist, and all those people who say they are true nonconformists are actually conformists just like the rest of us. How can you tell? Well, did you understand what they said? If so, then they aren't true nonconformists because they are conforming to the rules of language. Are they wearing clothes? Are they sitting on chairs? Total conformists. Imagine what life would be for a true nonconformist, or even worse, what life would be like around a nonconformist. No rules would apply. You would never know what to expect. Conformity is an absolute necessity for human survival. People have to be able to understand and interpret each other. People have to know how to behave and what to expect from their social environments. Conformity is what allows people to form social connections, create a culture, and live together. In short, it's part of being human.

The principle underlying conformity is the basic need for social connections. People are social animals and require relationships and social interactions to survive. We can't even have a true sense of self without social connections. Don't believe it? Try this simple test. Before you read any further, think of a list of ten words you would use to describe yourself. Write them down if you like. Did you come up with ten words? Do any of the words indicate a social position you occupy, for example, son, daughter, husband, mother? Or a social role, such as manager, director, leader? Did you have trait words, like generous, kind, smart, or funny? How about characteristics: Tall, brunette, or handsome? Words in any of the categories represent a social position. Even trait and character words. Why is one person tall? It's a relative term. That person is tall because he or she is taller than other people. What makes a person funny? No one is completely devoid of all sense of humor, but a person is considered funny is he or she is funnier than the average person.

The need for social interaction is a deep, primal need that exists in every person, no matter how independent he or she may like to be. We all need some social connections. Rebels are just people rejecting one group and joining another. The counterculture is not made up of nonconformists, but rather of individuals who reject the mainstream group in favor of a smaller group with different ideas and values.

Of course, in our culture, within the group, people want to be recognized individually. Within the safety of the group to which we belong, we want to be outstanding and unique.

NORMS

So what are we conforming to when we conform? We conform to social norms. *Norms* are rules about appropriate behavior, attitudes, beliefs, and values for a group. Norms can be formal or informal, explicit or implicit. In most societies, serious norms are formalized by laws. These are explicitly stated and violations of those norms are punished. *Mores* are less formal norms and represent less serious threats to social order when they are violated. Still, mores are associated with judgments of "right" and "wrong," and social disapproval will result from their violation. Folkways are routines of behavior: Customs, rituals, traditions, and the like. Violation of a folkway may earn you a stern look of disapproval, but not much more.

Organizations are like mini-societies in that they have formal laws or procedures that are written down and violations can be punished. It may be a violation of procedures to discuss confidential information in a public place, and violators may be reprimanded. Organizations also have mores and folkways. It may not be written down in a manual, but in an office of professionals, wearing a revealing blouse and a mini skirt might be seen as violating a more. Violating a folkway is as easy as sitting in the seat someone else always sits in during a staff meeting. Mores and folkways are often implicit, in other words, not formally stated. Yet, they are easily understood. For example, while not formally stated, you may simply understand that a Santa Claus tie won't be appreciated in your office, even if it is December.

Norms can also be injunctive or descriptive. Injunctive norms are beliefs about what people expect or approve of. Descriptive norms are beliefs about how people actually behave. For example, most people would agree that littering is not acceptable behavior. Throwing trash out of your car window, or throwing your Burger King bag in the parking lot would be perceived as behavior that violates the injunctive norm to refrain from littering. However, seeing a lot of trash alongside the road or in a parking lot suggests another norm. The descriptive norm would be that people actually do litter, as the trash attests.

The pull to conform to norms is incredibly strong. Try this simple experiment. Violate a folkway and see if you can feel the social pressure to conform. (It might be a good idea to do this away from the workplace.) If you don't want to actually do it, then imagine this situation. You're sitting at the table in a nice restaurant on a busy night with a few colleagues—and you are chewing with your mouth open. You know people are looking at you, then away from you. Are you able to imagine the disapproval you would feel emanating from everyone around you? Most of us would feel uncomfortable and possibly want to explain to any observers that we are just performing a little experiment, rather than have them think we are blatantly violating a social norm.

But here's an important point. You're able to imagine the social disapproval because you are aware of the norm you're violating by chewing with your mouth open. Norms are social constructions, created by groups, and therefore vary across groups. What is a violation for one group isn't necessarily for another, and members of one group may be completely unaware they are violating the norms of another. Ordering the wrong wine may turn a few heads in one group, and in another chewing gum with your mouth open doesn't get a second glance. Individuals won't feel the pressure to conform to group norms of which they are unaware although, when violating a norm, they sense that something isn't quite right.

PUBLIC CONFORMITY

One classic experiment demonstrates the strength of this pressure very well. Solomon Asch, in the early 1950s, conducted a series of experiments to investigate how people would respond to the pressure to conform in a group situation.[1]

Imagine you had signed up to participate in this study. You arrive at the lab and take the only remaining seat at a table with seven other students who are there, apparently to participate in the study too. The experimenter explains that the study is a test of visual perception. You are shown two cards like the ones in Figure 2.1 and asked to say aloud which one of the comparison lines is the same length as the standard line. The correct answer is clear. You are seated in the position to answer last, so you listen as everyone goes around the table giving the correct answer, and then you give your answer. More cards are shown, more answers given. Then, something strange happens. Two cards are shown with a clear correct answer, but you hear the other participants giving an answer that is wrong. The first student, then the second, then the third, all the way around the table are giving the same wrong answer. What do you do when it is your turn? Will you give the answer you know is correct? Or will you give the same answer as everyone else?

Several times during the session, all the other participants give an obviously wrong answer. What do you do? Would you give the wrong answer in order to be like the rest of the group? Would you do it every time? A few times? Not once?

In Asch's study, only 26% of the participants resisted the pressure to conform each and every time. Even though the task was unambiguous and they knew they were giving the incorrect answer, 66% conformed at least once.

This type of *public conformity* results from what is called normative influence. People gain information from the group about what is acceptable for group members, and then conform to those

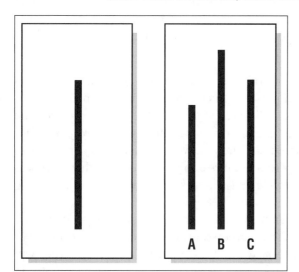

Figure 2.1

norms in terms of their outward behavior, although in private they might not adopt the norms. With public conformity, internalization of group norms is certainly possible, but it isn't required. People can be simply conforming outwardly to the group's norms in order avoid being alienated from the group.

PRIVATE CONFORMITY

In Asch's study, participants were motivated to give an incorrect answer to fit in with the group, but what would be different if the correct answer was unclear? In another classic study, this question was explored. In 1935, Muzafer Sherif examined the effects of group norms when the correct answer for a task was ambiguous.[2] For this study, participants looked at a pinpoint of light on a wall in a dark room and were asked to make judgments about how much the light was moving. In fact, the light wasn't actually moving, but it appeared to be, due to something called the autokinetic effect. The autokinetic effect is the result of the combination of the natural twitching in our eyes, our brain's expectation that our eyes are still, and the lack of reference points for the light because the room is dark.

In his study, Sherif asked groups of people to observe the movement of the pinpoint of light and then give several estimates of its movement. He asked people to make their first estimate when they were not able to hear each other. For the next three estimates, each participant was able to hear the estimates of the others. What do you think happened to the estimates each round? If you said they converged, you are right. Initial estimates typically showed wild variable, but by the third or fourth estimate, a group norm would emerge from the converging estimates.

In this case, the participants were using each other's estimates as valid information to help improve their own estimate. This is known as informational influence. There was no reason for participants to expect the information from each other to be flawed, so the participants were more likely to internalize the information or conform privately, as well as show their conformity in their behavior.

Notice the important differences between these two studies. In Asch's study the correct answer was obvious, the influence from the group was normative, and the public conformity resulted. In Sherif's study, the task was ambiguous and the correct answer was not known. (Indeed, the light was not actually moving.) The influence was informational, and the result was private conformity.

FACTORS THAT AFFECT THE DEGREE OF CONFORMITY

In the decades following the studies by Sherif and Asch, researchers have explored various factors affecting levels of conformity. Some of these studies were similar in design to Asch's original line study, but with some modification of a single variable, such as how many other participants were involved, to examine the effect of that variable on conformity. Those studies have revealed the following factors affecting conformity in group.

- **Number of people in group.** How does the number of other people in the group affect conformity? As you might expect, people feel increased pressure to conform when more people are in the group. Imagine if you and only one other person disagree about which line is the correct line in Asch's study. You'll probably feel little pressure to conform to the other person's way of thinking. But what if there are two others? What if there are three? Levels of conformity increase as the number of others increase, but this is true only to a point. At about five or six other members of the group, a point of diminishing returns is reached and adding more people doesn't increase levels of conformity that much more.
- **Ally in dissent.** What happens if one of the other members of the group refuses to conform? Imagine in Asch's study if one other member of the group dissents and gives the correct answer when everyone else is giving the obviously wrong answer. When your turn comes around, you will likely feel much less pressure to conform to the group because you already have an ally in dissent.

- **Public versus private responses.** People are also less likely to conform when their response is private. For example, in a jury poll the jurors in the minority will feel less pressure to conform to the majority if they are permitted to have a private response, like a secret ballot, versus public response.
- **Prior commitments.** A prior commitment to a position also reduces conformity. For example, let's say you have made it clear in conversations around the water cooler that a certain vendor, Vendor A, gives poor service and you are strongly in favor of using Vendor B. If, during a meeting to select a vendor for a new item, everyone else in the group is in favor of Vendor A, your prior commitment to Vendor B will make it less likely you will conform.

The pressure to conform and the factors that affect it have also been explored in research on a phenomenon called groupthink. *Groupthink* is experienced when members of a group all publicly conform to beliefs that they may privately disagree with. The result is poor decision-making processes and an increased likelihood of a poor, sometimes shockingly flawed decision.

Groupthink can occur in groups that are homogeneous, highly cohesive, and where membership is a status symbol. Group processes that contribute to groupthink include directive leadership, unsystematic procedures, and an open discouragement of dissension. The group is isolated from the outside, and feelings of invulnerability pervade the group. Symptoms of groupthink include close-mindedness, an overestimation of the group, and pressure to conform.[3]

Commonly referred to as "classic examples" of the groupthink, the Bay of Pigs invasion, the Watergate break-in, and the NASA Columbia and Challenger disasters illustrate how dreadful the consequences of groupthink can be. Fortunately, most examples of groupthink don't have the catastrophic and very public consequences as these. In organizations, it is easy to imagine how groupthink could occur, perhaps even frequently, on a much less publicly visible scale in the boardroom. Bad decisions that lead organizations to develop unmarketable products, to restructure in a way that destroys organizational culture, or to approve ads that offend the public are more like what everyday examples of the results of groupthink might look like.

Preventing groupthink is as simple as preventing the conditions that lead to it. Creating decision-making procedures for the group to follow is a good way to start. For example, assigning someone the role of devil's advocate for the group invites dissent rather than discouraging it. The role of the devil's advocate is to find fault with ideas and decisions and argue against the group. Even if the individual holding the role actually agrees with the group, he or she is required to find the flaws of the decision, opening the discussion for other group members.

GOING AGAINST THE GROUP: MINORITY INFLUENCE

In the 1957 movie *12 Angry Men*, Henry Fonda is part of a jury deciding the fate of a young man accused of killing his father.[4] In the beginning of the film, a vote is taken among the jury and 11 of the 12 vote "guilty." The only person voting "not guilty" is Henry Fonda. Initially, the 11 other jurors are convinced of the defendant's guilt and see no point in even deliberating the matter. The rest of the film depicts Fonda's struggle to encourage the rest of the members of the jury to consider the meaning of *beyond a reasonable doubt* and to question the conviction of the guilty judgment. This basic story has been repeated many times in television series and even situation comedies. The story's appeal speaks to the interest people have in standing against the group.

But in real life, does it pay to stand against the group? Let's refer back to the example of choosing between two suppliers: Vendor A and Vendor B. Let's assume that despite the desire of everyone else in the group wanting to go with Vendor A, you are convinced that Vendor B is the better choice. Is this simply a hopeless situation for you? Should you just give in and go with the group, or is there ever a time when the minority can have some influence on the majority? The minority can influence the majority in the group, especially under certain conditions. To be effective, minority member should be confident in the position, unwavering, and not have anything obvious to gain. In other words, if you confidently gave your reasons for wanting to go with Vendor B, and you didn't occasionally waffle and say that Vendor A wasn't that bad, and Vendor B is not owned by any of your relatives, then you could successfully bring the group around to seeing things your way.

CONFORMITY IN ORGANIZATIONS: ORGANIZATIONAL CULTURE

Every organization has a culture, a way things are done. The beliefs, attitudes, values, shared by the employees are part of the organizational culture. The jargon used, the political situation, the level of formality of communication, the rituals, the ceremonies, and more all contribute to culture, and likewise, are affected by culture. The use of physical space in an organization and the artifacts present communicate culture, as do behaviors.

When we begin working for an organization, we learn the culture and conform to it. Part of this orientation is accomplished through reading the required policies manual passed out by human resources, but adopting organizational culture necessitates much more than just that. We observe how things are done, notice what gets attention, listen to the stories told and attend the unspoken meanings behind the stories and, ultimately, learn to behave appropriately. Do employees address managers by their first name? Are personal pictures on all the desks? Is there art on the walls? Do managers leave their office doors open? Who gets the corner office? What department gets stuck in the basement? Understanding the culture of an organization requires analyzing all these things and more.

Managers need to consider organizational culture for two reasons. First, any significant change in an organization will encounter stumbling blocks if a corresponding cultural change is not planned. Mergers, like that of DaimlerChrysler, are a good example of large changes that frequently run into trouble because, despite the financial aspects of the deal being carefully scrutinized, important cultural challenges weren't considered. Chrysler's cultural values of creativity and egalitarian relationships were not shared by the DiamlerBenz culture that favored methodical decision making and formal channels of authority. These differing values translated into clashing work habits.[5] Second, employees will conform to the culture of the organizations they join. One of the considerations when selecting among job candidates (or for candidates, when choosing between job offers) is the "fit" between the organization and the person. Much of this goodness of fit is determined by how well a person can assimilate into the culture. For example, a stuffy introvert probably wouldn't enjoy working at Southwest airlines. Because employees will conform to the culture of the organization they join, managers have a great opportunity to influence the behaviors of employees simply by managing the organizational culture.

Creating the culture you want your employees to be part of involves assessing, changing, and strengthening organizational culture. Assessing organizational culture means analyzing the current culture and comparing it to the culture that would be necessary to accomplish the organization's goals. Whatever differences are discovered become the areas for change. Changing organizational culture is no easy task and will typically require one of three things: A crisis, a conversation, or an accumulation of small changes. A crisis or critical incident such as "firing everyone at the top" is not always desirable and may not be best way to create change because the outcome can be a little unpredictable. An open conversation about culture can work, but the size of the organization, characteristics of its members, or level of trust must be considered. This is not really an option for a large organization, one with employees of vastly different backgrounds or educational levels, or an organization in which management isn't trusted.

In most cases, the best way to create a change in culture is through small, cumulative changes. The following are focal areas that, when changed in concert, can have a significant impact on culture:

- **Policies and procedures.** Policies and procedures communicate a great deal about an organization's values and goals, and while they alone cannot completely change organizational culture, they can have a substantial impact. Consider the difference in culture between business schools with a forced grade distribution (i.e., only 20% of the class can receive an A, 20% must receive a C, and everyone else receives a B, and by the way, a C is considered failing) and a school without a forced distribution, wherein everyone in the class could conceivably receive an A in the class.

- **Rewards.** Make certain that behaviors that reflect the desired culture are rewarded and equally as important; avoid rewarding behaviors that don't. One MBA student complained that his family's business had a young female employee who always came to work 15 to 30 minutes late. His family had tried all sorts of things to get her to be on time, but nothing worked. When asked what the family had done, he replied that for a while someone was assigned to call the girl an hour before she was supposed to be at work, but that didn't work because she would fall back asleep. They had moved her start time in the morning from 9:00 a.m. to 9:30 a.m. since that was when she was getting to work anyway, but after that she just started showing up at 9:45. In this organization, the employee's undesirable behavior was being rewarded, but beyond that, the fact that it was being rewarded communicated something to everyone else about the culture of the organization.

- **Stories.** What stories do people tell about your organization? What stories do you tell? Stories are a way to pass along the history of the organization, the sources of pride, and the values of the organization. At one family-owned software company, the annual company party begins with story time. Managers from different departments tell stories, some of them funny, about different things their employees did for the company during the year. Story time always ends with the owner telling a story about starting the company. He tells jokes about the long hours and tight budget, and about the can-do attitude that led him and his partner, now deceased, to promise customers whatever they asked for and then scramble to figure out how to make those promises come true. His stories communicate to the employees the company's history, what it stands for and what it values. Managers need to tell the stories they want told.

- **Physical space.** A sound equipment company had seen three presidents come and go in less than a decade. In addition to losing leadership, they had begun to lose market share, and even long time customers—musicians with decades of loyalty to the company. The newest president was hired to pull the company out of its tailspin. One of the areas where he made significant improvement early on was in the repair division. Customers were able to send their products into the repair division, and they would be fixed and returned. But the repair division had become a chaotic pile of backlog. Items were sent in for repair and sat untouched on overfull shelves for two years. The first thing the new president did to improve the repair division was change the physical space. Everything was removed, the walls were painted a bright color, the floors were cleaned, lighting was improved, and everything was returned to the space in an orderly arrangement. This change to the physical space was all that was needed to turn the repair division around. But the change was more than just a new coat of paint. The change communicated that the company saw the repair division as important and that the division was a good place to work as well as a respectable place to be in the organization.

Organizational cultures can be either strong or weak. Organizations with strong cultures have employees whose decisions and behaviors are guided by a culture that is in alignment with the organizational goals. For these employees, the goals of the organization are internalized and shared by the employees. Organizations with weak cultures must use rules and procedures to tie behaviors to organizational goals. However, organizations can't rely completely on procedures to establish culture. Sometimes the formal norms of written procedures and the informal norms of how things are actually done will contradict one another. Managers may create formal policies and procedures that are all but ignored when it comes to how things are actually done in a weak culture. Strengthening organizational culture can be accomplished over time through socialization of employees. Creating opportunities to reinforce the culture of the organization might include an orientation session for new hires, maintaining rituals and traditions like company dinners, telling stories, as well as making formal statements of goals and the organization's mission. The modeling behavior of leaders is one of the most noteworthy ways to strengthen culture.

PERSUASIVE APPEALS TO CONFORMITY

Persuasive messages appeal to the need for acceptance by the group.

People who create persuasive messages such as advertising agents or salespeople are well aware of the deeply rooted need people have to be socially connected and accepted. Many advertisements appeal to the need to behave in an acceptable way, to look acceptable, or to join a group. Join the marines to be one of "the few, the proud." Brooke Shields invites you to "Join the Circle of Friends" to help people quit smoking.

Consider advertisements for beauty products that offer to protect you from wrinkles, save you from laugh lines, spare you from crow's feet, or promise simply to make you look younger. How are these messages playing on the principle of conformity? The answer lies in why someone would want to be saved from laugh lines. People in Western cultures do, because here youth is equated with beauty. The norm for beauty is tall, thin, and young. To the extent that we conform to this normative belief, we will see the aging process moving people further and further away from the valued standard of beauty. Judging from the ever-increasing number of anti-aging products available for both men and women, it appears that many of us are conforming to this norm.

Clever advertisers are also aware that we value independence in our culture and will therefore sometimes use *anti*-conformity appeals. These messages usually suggest that you should break away from the larger group—don't be like everyone else—and join a smaller group—be like us instead. In a recent Miller Lite ad, a group of men chant in unison what a member of the group should do, and some of the group's ideas aren't so great. At one point the group chants, "Hot sauce, hot sauce, hot sauce" while one character drinks hot sauce directly from the bottle. In another scene, the guys chant "Tribal armband, tribal armband" while one character gets his arm tattooed. At a bar, the group chants, "Beer, beer, beer, beer," and the bartender brings them all some unnamed brand of beer. She also gives a bottle to a young, handsome man standing nearby at the bar, but he stops her and says he wanted a Miller Lite. The narrator states something to the effect that sometimes it's better not to let your friends decide things for you. Clearly this is a message of nonconformity. What's funny, however, is that when the young man moves away from the bar back to his group of friends, they are all holding bottles of Miller Lite. The message of nonconformity advertisements isn't "don't conform;" it's actually "don't conform to that group, conform to our group instead."

OTHER GROUP EFFECTS

The influence of other people on individuals isn't limited just to conformity effects. Research on group influence shows a number of interesting group phenomena.

Group Polarization: Making decisions as a group. When groups make decisions, they tend to make decisions that are more extreme than the decisions of individuals in the group. Research in this areas typically involves having a group of people make a decision individually, then come together as a group, have a discussion, then repeat the decision making process, but this time as a group. At one time, it was believed that groups made what was called a *risky shift* during decision-making. In other words, a decision made by a group would involve a higher degree of risk than the same decision made by the same group of people individually.

Later research showed that this was an over-simplification of the process. In fact, groups tended to be moving to a more extreme position than their original position, but in the same direction as their original position, regardless of whether that move was toward more risk or more conservatism.[6] This shift actually makes sense if you consider a few explanations. First, it's likely that different members of the group have a variety of different reasons to hold their moderate position. After a discussion in which all those reasons are shared, each member now has additional information and reasons to intensify their original position. A second explanation has something to do with conformity. It could be that people grow more extreme in their position after learning that it is a socially accepted position. In other words, they initially hold back in the intensity of their position until learning that other people also feel the same way.

Social Facilitation: The presence of other influences us when we perform individually. Think about something you like to do and know you're very good at. Now think about something you don't have much experience doing and aren't good at. Which of these would you rather have an audience for? Most of us would prefer to be observed doing something we do well and avoid being observed when we are just learning how to do something or when we are doing something we find very difficult.

Think about these two tasks, jogging and dancing the rumba. Unless you're an experienced ballroom dancer, the rumba is probably going to be a challenge. You might be nervous about having people watch you as you struggle to remember the dance steps and coordinate your movements. In fact, you might be so nervous that the presence of others distracts you, and your performance suffers. On the other, if you are jogging in a 5K fundraiser, you might get your best time for that distance if you are running in front of a cheering crowd. Even if you feel a little nervous about people watching you run, that nervous energy is likely to fuel your performance and just make it better. You're not going to forget how to jog, but you might forget how to rumba if you're a novice.

This effect is called *social facilitation,* and it means that your performance on a familiar or easy task will improve with the presence of others, and that your performance on a novel or difficult task will decline in the presence of others. This is quite a robust finding and appears to apply to other creatures besides humans. In fact, even cockroaches show the social facilitation effect. Cockroaches that ran a complex maze in the presence of others (other cockroaches, not humans) took longer to complete the maze than those that ran the complex maze alone. On the other hand, cockroaches that ran a simple runway took less time when others were present than when alone.[7]

Social Loafing: Performing as a group. Does the presence of others always improve performance? Before you put everyone in your organization in a situation where all there work is done together in an attempt to take advantage of the social facilitation effect, consider the problem of *social loafing*. In some situations, working in a group can lead to individuals performing less well than they would alone. Classic studies of social loafing involved people pulling on a rope both individually and in groups, and the force on the rope was measured. It was determined that people pulled less hard on the rope when they were pulling as part of a group.

Social loafing appears to occur when individual effort is not identifiable, so making certain, to the extent possible, that individual performance within the group is determinable can be a good idea. Creating specialized roles for people within the group can increase accountability as well. Social loafing increases with the size of the group, so if group work is desired, smaller groups would be better. Of course, in situations where a group is highly cohesive or the task is important and meaningful to the group members, social loafing is less likely.

COMPLIANCE GAINING

Compliance is getting people to say yes to a request. Like public conformity, gaining compliance doesn't require internalization by the target of the message. In other words, getting people to say *yes*, even when they are not at all happy about it, counts as gaining compliance.

Your entire life you have been gaining compliance and using a number of strategies to do so. Consider the small child in the toy aisle who has spied a toy he simply must have. How can he get his parent to agree to buy that toy? First, he might simply ask, but if that fails ("No, Johnny, it's nearly your birthday."), he might move to plan B, maybe promising to be good or to clean his room when he gets home. If that fails, it might be time to bring out the heavy artillery: Begging, whining, crying, and throwing a complete fit. Observing small children in stores indicates this last technique works fairly well for many of them.

The point is, we all have many years of experience developing strategies for getting other people to do what we would like them to do. Most of those tactics would fall into one of these five categories:[8]

- **Rewards.** Offering a reward is a great way to get someone to do what you want them to do. We might take someone to lunch in exchange for a ride to the airport. We might promise to proofread a coworker's report if they will dig up an old file we need. Offering a reward needn't cost us much in terms of time or money because a reward is anything that the other person finds rewarding. A smile or a friendly conversation can be a reward. Rewards take two forms: The delivery of something pleasant (Giving your teenager twenty dollars for mowing the lawn) or taking away something unpleasant (Letting your teenager get out of mowing the lawn in reward for cleaning the garage).

■ **Punishments.** Punishments also come in two forms: The delivery of something negative (yelling at someone) or withholding something positive (giving someone the silent treatment). Anything that a person finds unpleasant is a punishment, and the desire to avoid being punished can lead someone to comply with a request.

■ **Expertise.** People with expertise or knowledge we don't possess can be very influential. For example, your doctor, or more importantly, your IT person, can gain compliance because of their expertise. However, the ability to use expertise is not limited to experts. Anyone can use the expertise of others to gain compliance. For example, you might cite the expertise of your IT person in your efforts to get someone to comply with you.

■ **Activation of commitments to self.** Here you are simply reminding someone of a commitment made to oneself to do a certain thing or act a certain way. For example, when you are trying to convince your colleague to stay late on Friday to get some work done, you might remind her of a commitment she made to avoid taking work home on the weekend.

■ **Activation of commitments to others.** In the situation above, you might activate a commitment to others by reminding your colleague of the commitment she made to her family to keep her weekends open.

These five general categories were developed by Marwell and Schmitt by grouping sixteen specific compliance-gaining tactics used in their research (see Table 2.1). It would be difficult to create a list of every tactic employed by people seeking compliance, but many of the more commonly used tactics appear on Marwell and Schmitt's list of sixteen.

Table 2.1   Marwell and Schmitt's sixteen compliance-gaining tactics and examples of how they might be used to get someone to buy a gym membership:

1. **Promise:** A reward is promised to the person in return for compliance.
   If you join the gym, I'll create a personalized program just for you to help you meet your fitness goals.

2. **Threat:** A punishment will result if the person does not comply.
   If you don't join the gym today, I can't guarantee this offer of special pricing later.

3. **Expertise (positive):** Good things will happen as a result of compliance "because of the nature of things."
   If you join the gym you'll have more energy and look better because exercise improves your health.

4. **Expertise (negative):** Bad things will happen as a result of a refusal to comply "because of the nature of things."
   If you don't exercise and take care of yourself, your health will deteriorate.

(Continued)

Table 2.1   (*Continued*)

5. **Liking:** The compliance seeker demonstrates liking of the target and may offer praise.

   To sell a gym membership the salespeople will smile, act interested in the customer, and offer compliments and encouragement.

6. **Pre-giving:** A reward is given before compliance is sought.

   Gyms frequently offer a free trial period and one free visit with a personal fitness consultant before asking the target to purchase a full membership.

7. **Aversive stimulation:** An unpleasant or punishing situation is created that ends when the target complies.

   After an initial meeting salespeople will call the target repeatedly to ask if they are ready to join the gym.

8. **Debt:** Past favors create a debt that can be paid back by compliance.

   During a free introductory visit to the gym, a salesperson will spend a great deal of time focused on the target, showing the target how to use all the machine, weighing and measuring the target, talking to the target about fitness and creating an exercise plan just for the target.

9. **Moral appeal:** An appeal is made that noncompliance is somehow immoral.

   You're given one body and it's only right to take care of it.

10. **Self-feeling (positive):** Targets are told they will feel good about themselves if they comply.

    You are going to feel so proud of yourself when you start getting in shape.

11. **Self-feeling (negative):** Targets are told they will feel bad about themselves if they don't comply.

    If you don't start working out, you're just going to feel more frustrated and disappointed with yourself.

12. **Altercasting (positive):** The target is told a person with desirable qualities would comply.

    Success oriented people like to belong to a gym.

13. **Altercasting (negative):** The target is told a person with undesirable qualities would not comply.

    Your average couch potato wouldn't be interested in joining our gym.

14. **Altruism:** Compliance is requested for the sake of helping out the compliance seeker.

    If I sell one more gym membership this month, I win a free dinner for two.

15. **Esteem (positive):** Targets are told that other people will think better of them if they comply.

    Your significant other is going to think you look great after you've been working out for a while.

16. **Esteem (negative):** Targets are told that other people will think worse of them if they don't comply.

    Your family will be upset if you let you health deteriorate.

Note: When selling gym memberships, salespeople often talk about "buying the gym membership" and "working out" as if they are the same thing even though the salespeople know they aren't the same at all. Many people buy memberships and sign long contracts and end up not actually using the gym, but the sales language doesn't distinguish between buying and using.

With so many options available, how do you decide which tactic to use when you are attempting to gain compliance? Well, for starters, most of the time you employ a combination of tactics. For example, if you need a colleague's assistance you might ask for help, give a promise of something you can do in the future (Promise), and act like you like the person (Liking), and let the person know how much everyone else in your department will appreciate the person's effort (Esteem, positive).

The particular combination of tactics you use to gain compliance in a given situation will be affected by a number of things including the importance of your request, the nature of the relationship, the power distribution between you and the other person, how likely it is that the person will comply, the consequences to the relationship if a certain tactic is used, and so forth. In other words, you probably wouldn't use Threat with a person more powerful than you, and you're not likely to use Esteem Negative or Aversive Stimuli if your relationship with a client might be damaged.

CIALDINI'S SIX PRINCIPLES OF INFLUENCE

Robert Cialdini, a social psychologist from Arizona State University, has spent decades studying compliance gaining strategies. In his immensely popular book, *Influence*, he describes six principles of social influence that he has researched both in the lab and in the field. These six principles have been repeatedly shown to increase levels of compliance.[9]

Reciprocity. It happens at work all the time. One of your colleagues pops into your office selling cookies or candy from their child's school, scouting group, or little league team. Of course, you don't want to by any overpriced candy or overly processed cookies (unless they are Girl Scout cookies, which are truly delicious), but if you don't buy, what will happen next week when you try to sell gift wrap for *your* child's soccer club? If you buy from your colleague today, your colleague is more likely to buy from you next week. This is an example of reciprocity at work. The principle of reciprocity is the rule that we should repay what has been done for us. Cialdini tells the story of a university professor who tried a little experiment. One year he sent a number of Christmas cards to perfect strangers just to see what would happen.[10] The response he got was a flood of cards in return from people who had no idea who he was. The people who sent those cards couldn't receive a card from someone without sending one back, even if they didn't have a clue who the sender was. This story illustrates the strength of the principle of reciprocity.

This rule of reciprocity is a powerful force that, unlike many social forces that are tied to a particular culture, seems to operate universally. Cialdini tells how he was surprised to find that in 1985, Ethiopia, a nation suffering from abject poverty with thousands dying from disease and starvation, sent $5,000 in aid to Mexico after the earthquake that rocked Mexico City. It turns out that Ethiopia was returning a favor done by Mexico in 1935 when Mexico had sent aid to Ethiopia after it had been invaded by Italy.

The principle of reciprocity has already been captured and applied in professional endeavors. Nonprofits seeking donations through the mail provide a good example. If you move to a new address, you will receive a windfall of address labels in the mail from various charitable organizations hoping you will send them a donation in return for their small gift. In the fall, you may receive calendars in the mail from organizations seeking donations. Marketing research firms might send you a crisp, new dollar bill in the envelope with a survey they ask you to complete. Can you feel good about spending that dollar if you don't reciprocate and complete the survey?

Through the principle of reciprocity, doing things for others can be a great strategic move. It creates future indebtedness, so we can all become like the Godfather, with favors owed to us that we can use later when we need them. Of course, the rule works both ways. If you accept favors from others, you can feel an obligation to them. You can feel like you "owe" them. This is true even for unwanted or uninvited favors, like the address labels.

The rule of reciprocity works because of perceptions of favors and debt. If these perceptions don't form, the principle won't work. If you have done a favor for a colleague and have spent a great deal of time and effort on whatever it is, when the person thanks you for your help, how do you respond? Many of us might respond with a comment that discounts or diminishes all the work we have just done. We might say, "It was nothing" or "No problem" or "Think nothing of it." The danger, or course, is that the other person might do just that—think nothing of it—and then our future debt to be paid doesn't exist. Of course, it probably won't get us very far to hold a debt over someone's head: "You owe me and you better be ready to pay up." That could be perceived as inappropriate or rude and could provide justification for a lack of reciprocation. Cialdini recommends responding with something like, "I know you'd do the same for me."

Sometimes the rule of reciprocity can fail because we do things for others that are not seen as favors or as sacrifices or extra effort on our part. Possibly the other person simply doesn't understand what's involved for us. For example, the accountant at a small company was frequently asked by the sales manager for the favor of preparing various special reports. Every few months, the sales manager would ask for some type of report, and each one took time out of the accountant's day and sometimes made him behind in his regular work. At the same time, when the accountant would ask the sales manager for some small favor, such as getting in expense reports early, the sales manager never complied. The problem was that the sales manager thought the reports he was asking for were easily accessible: Common reports that would take no extra effort to prepare; therefore, he never saw his request as a way of incurring debt to the accountant. We might have to explain at some point exactly what it is we are doing, so that person can understand a debt is being created.

Commitment and consistency. People want to appear consistent, and if people take a stand or make a public commitment, they are likely to stick to it. A written commitment is one of the strongest sorts of commitment available. If you are trying to get commitment from your employees, or even from yourself, get it in writing if possible. Importantly, though, commitments must be voluntary. A commitment that is forced upon an employee is not really a commitment but rather a burden that is likely to lead to resentment and contrary behavior when possible, such as when the boss is away.

Consensus or social proof. According to Cialdini, the principle of social proof says that *"we view a behavior as correct in a given situation to the degree that we see others performing it."*[11] We often find advertisers using phrases indicating social proof in ads, such as "95% of people agree," "most popular," "everyone's talking about" or "largest selling." Nonprofits use social proof in fundraising shows where they instruct people calling in to give donations to call back if lines are busy, indicating that others are calling. During the fundraising week on the local public radio station, listeners are invited to call in to donate and the names of people in the community who have just made a donation are read. As we determined in our discussion on conformity, group norms can be highly influential. Social proof of what other people are doing, especially similar others or peers, can be persuasive.

Organizations can use the principle of social proof in advertising or fundraising. Internally, managers can use the principle of social proof to create change within the organization. Of course, managers are not always the ones employees look to for social proof. If managers are not considered to be similar to employees and to share the same goals, then arguing "All the managers in your organization agree…" might not be a persuasive piece of social proof. Winning over opinion leaders to whom employees look for guidance about how to respond can be a better strategy.

Social proof can work even when we don't want it to. People do what they perceive others to do even when it isn't desirable behavior. Suicides increase immediately after the story of a suicide appears in the press. Copycat crimes occur and people commit crimes that emulate what they observe in movies. Despite warnings on television shows like *Jackass* telling viewers explicitly that they will get hurt if they try the stunts they are about to see, viewers at home still try them and they do get hurt. Organizations need to be mindful of the consequences of their messages of social proof.

Liking. When people like us, we are more likely to like them. When people like us and we like them, we want to be nice to them and make them happy. This means increased levels of compliance.

But why do people like each other and how can we get people to like us better? We tend to like people we have something in common with, people we feel are similar to us in some way. Managers can develop stronger relationships with employees by finding common interests and focusing on similarities. People also tend to like people who offer them praise: Not artificial, obviously contrived, Eddie Haskell type of praise ("That dress is very becoming on you, Mrs. Cleaver.") but genuine, sincere praise. Managers can use positive comments about employees to build, or possibly repair, relationships with them.

Authority. Expertise can be persuasive. And why not? In a world where available information increases at a ferocious rate, the average person needs the guidance of experts in making decisions. People can be misled by experts, certainly, but the use of expertise is undeniable. You can increase your influence by making sure people are aware of your credentials, and you should do this before you attempt to influence others. Your credentials aren't going to make you more influential if no one knows about them. That doesn't mean arrogantly boasting about them but rather subtly making them known. For example, diplomas can be hung on an office wall; when giving a presentation, important credentials can be revealed during an introduction; in conversation, it might be possible to touch on a problem you solved in the past; and, of course, credentials should be mentioned in your company biography. Subtlety is called for, but most people want to know how to judge the quality of the information they are getting, and your credentials are part of that. They want to know if you are an expert.

Compliance to authority does have a dark side. When we don't understand what someone with credentials is saying or when we feel that person has more status or expert power than us, we may take the mental shortcut of deferring to expertise instead of critically evaluating arguments and then deciding. Studies with doctors and nurses illustrate this problem. In one study, staff nurses alone at the nursing station in the evening received a call from an unknown voice. The man on the phone claimed to be a doctor and directed the nurse to administer a large dose of an unfamiliar drug to the doctor's patient on that ward. The doctor said he would be there in a few minutes but wanted the drug to be taking effect by the time he arrived. Over 95 percent of the nurses in the study were on their way to administer the drug to the patient when they were stopped in the hall and told it was just an experiment.[12]

Scarcity. Imagine you are at the store looking at an item and considering purchasing it. You don't need it, but you want it. You would like to wait and think about it a little more, but it appears to be the last one left. Will the fact that it's the last one influence your decision to purchase the item? Cialdini would say it probably will. When something is scarce, it becomes more desirable, more valuable, and precious. As Cialdini says, *people want more of what they can have less of.*

This is not news to people creating advertisements, letting you know that a price is good only while supplies last, or that limited quantities are available, or a sale is in its "final week." QVC shows the number of items left in inventory ticking down as the items are purchased by callers. (The double whammy: Social proof and scarcity.)

The principle of scarcity doesn't apply only to tangible items, but to information as well. If there is a juicy little tidbit going around the office, but only a few people know about it, how much more thrilling is that than the piece of information sent out in a companywide e-mail.

Cialdini's principles can work in tandem as well and independently to increase compliance. Think about the social influence involved when you attend a Pampered Chef® party or a ProShop@Home party. If you want to buy new cooking equipment or a new set of golf clubs, you can do it online; you don't have to go to a party. When the invitation to a Pampered Chef party arrives in the mail, you can feel yourself fill with dread. If the invitation is from someone you like, even a little bit, you have to go or come up with a good excuse not to. Then, if you go, bring your checkbook because you know you will buy something. It doesn't matter if you don't need anything, it almost doesn't matter what the products are: You know you will buy something because you don't want to disappoint your friend. And, not only will you disappoint your friend who is hosting the party if you don't place an order, but now there is this very knowledgable representative you've just met, who is so sweet and friendly and *loves* these products and is so enthusiastic about them, you can't imagine not buying something, especially after she's just cooked some delightful appetizers for you. Besides, everyone else at the party is ordering something.[13]

And why do you think your friend had that Pampered Chef party? Was it just because she wanted the free hostess gift? That's doubtful. Somewhere down the line of parties conducted by this sales representative is the friend or relative that let her do her first party at her house. It probably began with a phone call from the brand new sales rep asking for "help" since she was just starting out and needed a "safe" place to throw her first party. Then, of course, she would ask all of her best friends and relatives to give her contact information for other people who might want to have a party at their house, and so on. So, even the request to have the party probably came from a friend or from a person given the contact information by another friend. The free Pampered Chef items for the hostess just make it harder to turn down. And why turn it down anyway? After all, you've been to several similar parties at your friends' homes, so . . . don't they owe you something?

SEQUENTIAL REQUEST STRATEGIES

Sequential request strategies involve seeking compliance by asking more than one question in such a way that the first question increases the level of compliance to the second request. Sequential request strategies rely on the principles of *context* and *contrast effects*. We use *anchor points* to establish context when we make decisions. In other words, we employ a psychological backdrop against which we judge things. We quickly acclimate to new backdrops or anchor levels and then judge against those new levels. You might, for example, be able to get your teenager to mow your lawn for ten dollars until he gets a job and starts receiving a paycheck. After that, ten dollars might not seem like enough to get him interested.

Using a decoy is an example of creating a contrast effect. Realtors might show a property they know their client won't want first just to make the next property look that much better. Price changes can create contrast effects. A discount or price drop can lead people to buy. Wal-Mart makes sure to point out lower prices. However, lower prices have to be a perceived as a noticeable difference to create a reaction. For example, the owner of one specialty retail store was told by a sales representative from a local radio station not to even bother to advertise a 10% off sale because it's not a large enough discount to mean anything to anyone anymore. The price that is 10% lower might not be a noticeable difference in price, but the percentage off is definitely a noticeably minor difference for shoppers accustomed to 40% of 50% off. A mere 10% hardly seems like a discount. Examples of several well-known sequential request strategies are found readily in everyday messages.

The door-in-the-face technique. The door-in-the-face technique involves asking for something very large with the first request, and then something smaller with the second request. This strategy is popular with public television stations during fundraisings. They will start their request for a donation by saying that you can become a platinum member with a donation of $5000 and a gold member with a donation of $1000. They might then talk about donating $365 ("That's just a dollar a day!") and eventually work their way down to $50 or even just $20. Most people aren't going to give $5000 and the public television station is well aware of that. However, more people will give $100 or $50 if the station starts out by asking for much more.

Cialdini explains this through his principle of reciprocity. He suggests that the requester is making a concession by lowering the amount of the request. The responder then feels the need to reciprocate. This idea of reciprocal concessions works only when the requests closely follow each other. If too much time goes by, the second request, even though it is for less, will be seen as a new request.

The foot-in-the-door technique. The reverse process is also known to increase levels of compliance to the second request. In this case, a small request is made first, followed by a larger request. For example, you may get a call from someone doing a telephone survey. The person asks if you would be willing to answer a few questions about your radio listening habits. You're told the survey will take less than five minutes, so you say yes. Indeed, only a few questions are asked and the survey takes less than five minutes. At the end of the survey, however, the person asks if it would be okay if you received a call in the next few weeks to complete another survey which would last about fifteen minutes. Since you have already said yes to the first request about the short interview, you are more likely to say yes to the second request than you would be if this request for fifteen minutes of your time came out of the blue.

Cialdini offers an explanation for this finding based on his principle of commitment. People like to appear consistent and, if you have said yes to the first request, it would seem inconsistent to then say no to the second.

Low-balling. Low-balling is a term used in several different ways. In the area of sequential requests, it refers to the tactic of getting someone to say "yes" to a request and then escalating the cost of that compliance. An episode of the *I Love Lucy* show illustrates this process perfectly when Lucy is visited by a door-to-door salesman selling the latest, greatest canister vacuum. Lucy isn't supposed to spend money on a vacuum, but of course, she buys it. She committed to buying the vacuum for the price the salesman gave her, but then she learns that the hose costs extra and all the attachments and gadgets cost extra. By the time the transaction is finished Lucy has spent a small fortune and knows that she's going to have some "splainin to do" when Ricky gets home. Naturally, she and Ethel decide to go door-to-door to sell the vacuum to someone else, so Lucy can get the money back before Ricky finds out, and hilarity ensues. The point of the story is that Lucy committed to one price for the vacuum and then found the cost was actually much higher. Serious ethical concerns are associated with low-balling.

That's not all. Another very common strategy is the "That's not all" technique. Anyone who's watched television past midnight has seen this technique in action. "You can get all these kitchen knives for $19.95. But wait! There's more! You can also get this carrot peeler. And that's not all. If you order now, we'll include this potato masher. All this for just $19.95." The original offer might have seemed fair, but after everything has been added to it, it seems too good to pass up.

OBEDIENCE

Compliance-gaining strategies are used to get someone to say "yes" to a direct request. But sometimes a request isn't really a request at all. It's an order phrased as a question. Obedience differs from compliance in the lack of perception of choice. Obedience is the response to a directive, rather than a request, by another. Most people equate obedience with a perception of little or no choice. Others (mostly undergraduates studying philosophy) like to argue that people always have a choice. The argument goes something like this:

Instructor: Your boss comes in your office on Friday afternoon and says you have to work late. And you do.

Student: Well, you didn't *have to* work. You could have opted to tell your boss no and take the consequences, even if you got fired. You could have made the choice to get fired. It's not like your boss had a gun to your head.

Instructor: Okay. Let's say you're crossing the dark, empty parking lot on you way to your car, after working late on Friday, and a mugger comes out of nowhere, holds a gun to your head and says, "Give me your wallet." And you do.

Student: Well, I think you still have a choice. You are *choosing* not to get shot and to give your wallet to the mugger.

And so on . . . So again, obedience involves a *perception* of a lack of choice. Where that perceptual line between choice and no choice is drawn varies from person to person.

Perhaps the most famous work on the subject of obedience was conducted by Stanley Milgram, a Yale professor, in the early and mid 1960s.[14] Milgram was interested in the events of World War II and rejected the idea that the atrocities of the war could be explained by saying the Germans were bad people. He considered the power of the situation and wondered if people did things during the war that they didn't want to do but felt they had little power to resist given the situation. He wondered what aspects of the situation could contribute to people doing what they would never imagine themselves capable of.

To study this question, he set up an experiment at Yale. He put an advertisement in the local paper looking for research subjects, men between the ages of 20 and 50, for a study about memory and learning. The respondents to the ad comprised a mix of age, education, and income levels.

Imagine if you responded to the ad, you would be instructed where to go and when. When you arrive at the lab, you are asked complete some questionnaires and sign some papers. You are paid the $4.50 promised in the ad, and then led to another room to wait for the experiment to start. The room is a small lab with a large machine that fills an entire desktop. A book on theories of learning rests on top of the machine. A gentleman, another subject you presume, is also waiting. You don't know it, but this man is actually a confederate, a person who works for the experimenter but poses as just another subject. Finally, the experimenter enters the room. He's wearing a white lab coat and has a serious demeanor. He tells you a little bit about the experiment: "Psychologist have developed several theories to explain how people learn various types of material . . . One theory is that people learn things correctly whenever they get punished for making a mistake."[15]

The experimenter goes on to say that very little is known about the effects of punishment on learning, for example "how much punishment is best for learning" or what effects the characteristics of the person giving the punishment have on learning, and so forth.

He then explains that in the current study, one of you will be the teacher and one of you will be the learner. He asks you to select one of the two small, folded papers from his palm, explaining that this is a fair way of assigning one of you to the role of teacher and one of you to the role of learner. You unfold your paper and you read teacher. You don't know it, of course, but both papers read "teacher." You are initially relieved to see that you have been assigned the role of teacher. After all, the learner is going to get punished and that doesn't sound fun.

The experimenter says that it's time to set the learner up to receive the punishment. You're invited to come along to see how this is done. In an adjacent room, you observe the learner's arms being strapped to the arms of a chair. The experimenter explains this is necessary to prevent excessive movement when the learner is being shocked. He then attaches a small electrode to the learner's wrist with some electrode paste "to avoid blisters and burns." The electrode is ostensibly connected to the large machine in the other room, which you now learn is a shock generator.

At around this point, the learner reveals that he was recently diagnosed with a heart condition and asks the experimenter about the danger of the shocks. The experimenter indicates that the shocks are painful, but not dangerous.

You are now feeling really glad that you are in the teacher's role, but that doesn't last long. You follow the experimenter back into the other room where he acquaints you with the shock apparatus. The machine sits on top of a table. As you sit before it, you observe that it has knobs across the top and levers corresponding to different levels of shock that span the entire width of the machine. The levers are labeled with voltage level of the shock, starting at 15 volts and increasing by increments of 15 all the way up to 450 volts. The shock levels are also labeled with a verbal description. Levels 15 volts through 60 volts are labeled "Slight Shock," levels 75 to 120 are labeled "Moderate Shock" and so on, all the way up to a classification of "Danger: Severe Shock" and finally, just an ominous "XXX."

The experimenter explains that you, communicating through a microphone and speaker system in the machine, will read a list of word pairs to the learner. The learner is to try to remember the word pairs and when prompted by you with the first word of each pair, must supply the second word. If he does, great! Move on to the next word. If not, you must punish the learner by pulling a lever and giving him a shock, and with each incorrect answer the level of the shock will increase.

Then, you're asked if you wouldn't mind getting a sample shock yourself because it's only fair that you know what the learner is experiencing. You roll up your sleeve and receive a sample shock, which, by the way, hurts a bit, though you are told that it was a mild-level shock.

The experimenter then instructs you to begin. At this point, you have to make a decision. Are you going to administer painful shocks to the person in the other room or not?

For participants in Milgram's study, the first few trials proceeded uneventfully. The learner got some of the word pairs correct and some incorrect. For the incorrect responses, the learner received a shock. At first, the learner showed no signs of discomfort in response to the shocks, but started to respond with a little grunt at 75-volts. After that, as the voltage increases, the responses intensified from painful groans, banging on the wall, refusals to cooperate any longer, to cries for help and agonizing screams. After 330-volts, the learner suddenly becomes completely quiet and is heard from no more.

If at any time during the experiment the participant turned to the experimenter for help, to ask if the study should be stopped, or to ask the experiment to check on the learner, the experimenter would respond with several prompts, including "Please go on" or "It is absolutely essential that you continue."

Imagine what is going through the mind of the participant as this drama unfolds. No doubt they have a real concern for the well-being of the learner, and in fact, might even wonder if the learner is still alive after he falls silent. How would you respond if you were one of Milgram's participants? You probably think you would have told the experimenter "no way" at some point early on in the experiment. Perhaps you would have refused to participate as soon as you learned that you would have to give another person shocks, or perhaps you would quit as soon as it was apparent the learner was suffering some discomfort. Indeed, when Milgram asked 110 respondents who heard a description of the study what they thought they would do, all 110 indicated that they would disobey the experimenter at some point and refuse to continue the study. Very few indicated they would continue past the first signs of the learner's pain.

But in actuality, Milgram's found 65% of the participants were obedient to the experimenter, shocking the learner despite his agonizing cries and pleas to be released, pulling each lever all the way to the end of the board, and continuing to shock the learner with the final lever marked "XXX 450 volts" several times before the experiment was finally ended. The results were surprising, even to Milgram.

So what happened? Did Milgram's ad mistakenly run in the *Evil Doers Daily*? Hardly. Participants in Milgram's study were just average people, like anyone else. Even the participants who obeyed the experimenter to 450 volts protested and expressed their concern about the learner. They were uncomfortable and visibly agitated. Yet, despite their discomfort, they acted obediently.

The primary difference Milgram found between obedient and disobedient participants was the amount of responsibility they assumed for the learner's suffering. Disobedient participants were likely to see themselves as more responsible for the learner's suffering than the experimenter and to assign the learner very little responsibility for his plight. The obedient participants, on the other hand, were likely to see the experimenter as slightly more responsible than themselves for the learner's torment and to assign the learner a significant share of the responsibility for his own suffering.

Milgram conducted variations of his experiment to explore which aspects of the situation contributed to participants being obedient. Some of those variations and the results follow:

- The experiment was conducted in an office building instead of on the campus of Yale, resulting in 47.5% of the participants being obedient to the experimenter.
- An ordinary man gave the orders in one variation instead of an experimenter in a lab coat. This resulted in 20% obedience.
- In one variation, the experimenter left the room after giving instructions and gave orders by phone, with a result of 20.5% obedience.
- Two peers rebelled against the experimenter and that defiance was witnessed by the participant, after which 10% were obedient.
- The participants chose the level of shock delivered in one variation and only one person out of 40 used the highest level of shock. The great majority used only the lowest levels on the board.

The variations on Milgram's study indicate two things quite clearly. The expertise or perceived power of the experimenter was a significant contributor to the resulting obedience, and if people believed they had their choice, they would not have hurt the learner. So why did people obey the experimenter, when clearly they would rather not have? They were paid $4.50, a small enough amount that this would not be an incentive; furthermore, they received the money at the beginning of the experiment and were told it was theirs to keep no matter what happened. There was no real threat of reprisal if they refused the experimenter. They weren't going to get fired or anything of that sort. So, in the absence of incentives or threats, people obeyed a malevolent authority commanding them to act in violation of their desires and values.

Milgram offered the explanation that we are socialized to follow legitimate authority. People wanted to please the experimenter, to be "good subjects," so they continued to obey even as the experimenter led them step-by-step into behaviors they would never choose for themselves.

The relevance today of Milgram's study of destructive obedience is seen in the scandals of recent years, involving Abu Ghraib, Tyco, Enron, WorldCom, and others. Perhaps, this shouldn't be surprising. If people will obey legitimate authority for no other reason than to be good subjects, how likely will they be to obey when defiance could result in real retaliation? When your boss says to "meet the quarterly earnings goals" or "make the numbers" or "fix it," an enormous amount of pressure comes to bear. In organizations with not only the desire to be seen "as a good subject" operating, but the fear of being perceived as not being a team player and the very real impact that might have on one's career, the threat of excessive obedience is quite real. Most of us would like to believe that when we are faced with an ethical dilemma, we can rely on our conscience and our values to guide our behavior, but Milgram's studies show that we can't take this for granted when faced with powerful situational demands.

In Milgram's experiment, the participants frequently asked the experimenter to check on the subject or if they should stop the experiment. More familiar in organizations are examples of obedience that don't involve vigorous protests or lots of questions. More likely are hints of concern or questions that dance around an issue. For example, an article in the *Journal of Aviation/Aerospace Education and Research* estimates that up to 20% of all airplane accidents could be prevented if first officers would monitor the captain and challenge captain errors. Instead of directly questioning or challenging the captain, first officers are likely to ask only indirect questions and may not even attempt to monitor situations or problem solve because authority and responsibility are deferred completely to the captain.[16]

The consequences of destructive obedience won't typically be an Enron-type scandal or a fatal plane crash although sometimes they will be. The consequences might be a fudged number or two on a report, a document signed that wasn't read, a product that was allowed to ship when it shouldn't have, a machine that continues to run when it represents a danger to production workers. Consider the experience of J.D., a young production worker who tells the story of a visit two "suits" from the corporate office made to the plant where he worked after a complaint of an OSHA violation was made. At this particular facility, cargo trailers are customized. J.D. worked in final finish, which involved painting, cleaning, and sealing the interior of each trailer. Because the workers in final finish used chemicals with dangerous fumes inside the trailers with very little ventilation, they were required to wear masks and a fan was to be blowing at all times to increase the airflow. However, the masks made it difficult to see, they were hot, and the masks slowed production, so the production manager didn't make the employees wear them. And because there was only one fan at the facility, the finish group frequently didn't have a fan blowing where they were working. One day, a woman who had been with the company working in final finish got upset about something and stormed out of the plant. She went to her car to leave, then changed her mind, turned around, and tried to come back to work. But the production manager told her she was fired for walking out. The woman got angry and called the corporate office to report the safety violations in final finish. The next day two people from the corporate office pulled into the parking lot. They entered the plant through the front office and, while they were chatting with the general manager, the production manager moved into action. He instructed a worker to move the large fan to final finish and turn it on while he unlocked the closet where the masks were stored and made everyone put on a mask. He told them how to bend the mask around the bridge of their nose so it would look broken. Then he called the seven final finish employees together and told them that they would probably be asked some questions about how things were done there, and they needed to tell the corporate people that they always had a fan and they always wore a mask. The seven employees were interviewed individually, and each one of them took their turn telling a lie about the masks and fan. J.D. reported not wanting to lie but feeling as if he didn't have a choice.

It's worthwhile to note that excessive obedience can be an artifact of the directive style of the leader, the culture of the organization, and the systems and procedures in place. Destructive obedience isn't always the objective of the one being obeyed. A pilot on a collision course would prefer to be corrected.

Organizations need to protect managers and employees from the risk of destructive obedience, intended or unintended. Pressure, stress, and legitimate authority all contribute to excessive obedience but are all an inevitable part of organizational life that can't be changed. It's possible, however, that through training, creating an open organizational culture, and putting in place systems and procedures that encourage communication, the opportunity for destructive obedience can be reduced, if not eliminated. Researchers studying the problem of obedience in first officers suggested training first officers to challenge captains by putting them through exercises where captains make planned mistakes and then evaluating the first officer's response.

WHEN TO SEEK OBEDIENCE

Obedience in the workplace is common and not without its proper place. The problem with obedience comes when excessive obedience is produced and real concerns aren't voiced, as we have discussed. The other problem with giving orders and expecting obedience is when it becomes a default method of influence. Today, with flattened organizational structures and the free flow of information, the talented employee has little patience for unquestioned authority. People want to understand why they are doing what they are doing, and they may have their own ideas about what ought to be done and how. They want to feel as if they have a voice and that it is respected. The "because I said so" reasoning doesn't set any better with your direct reports than it did with you when your parents used it.

Using obedience doesn't produce lasting change that continues after your back is turned. When people feel like they can disobey an order, but not get caught, many of them will disobey. Consider what happened in one of the versions of Milgram's study. In this variation, after the experimenter gave the initial instructions to the teacher, he left the room and delivered the rest of his orders by phone. This meant that the experimenter was not able to observe what the teacher was doing. Not only did the number of participants who obeyed the experimenter to the end drop to 20.5%, many of the participants gave the learner lower levels of shock than were required by the experimenter. Some even lied to the experimenter, assuring him that they were giving the higher levels of shock.

There is a time and a place for seeking obedience, but recognize its limitations and use it sparingly. The following are examples of times would obedience would a reasonable choice of social influence:

- **When a decision/action must be executed that is unfavorable but necessary.** Not every decision a manager makes is going to be popular. You will likely make some decisions that have a negative impact on some employees, especially in difficult times.
- **When a decision/action is required quickly.** Sometimes you just need your people do what you tell them to do, no questions asked, because that is all that time allows. In a moment of crisis, you may not have time for discussion or to make a good argument, you might just tell people what you need them to do and expect them to do it.
- **When you have the expertise and others don't.** You may not always need or want to explain your reasoning to someone who doesn't have your knowledge base.

A final question when it comes to seeking obedience is the ethics involved in this choice. If you have authority over another person, when is it unethical to use forcing strategies to get obedience? Perhaps when you force them to do something they don't want to do. What about the Michigan company that gave its employees a year to quit smoking or be fired because of the cost to the business associated with healthcare of smokers? Is that unethical? Perhaps it's forcing someone to do something they feel is wrong. What about the pharmacist who doesn't believe in birth control yet is told he must fill prescriptions for birth control or lose his job? Is that unethical? Referring back to the TARES test from Chapter One may help us determine when an order we expect others to follow is unethical. In many ways, just asking the question of whether our communication is ethical is our best defense against making an unethical demand.

In this chapter we have discussed forms of social influence that are common and effective ways of influencing others but fall short of what we have defined as true persuasion. In the next chapter we move beyond tactics for getting the behaviors we want from others, and begin our discussion of creating internalized change through building a persuasive argument.

DISCUSSION QUESTIONS

1. Discuss the culture of your most recent employer or your school? What elements communicate the culture? What would you change? How would you do it?

2. Based on what you've read in this chapter, why do you think "the Good Cop/Bad Cop" routine works?

3. How would you use the sixteen different compliance gaining tactics proposed by Marwell and Schmitt to get your employees to contribute to their retirement account?

4. How does the use of obedience affect organization culture?

ENDNOTES

1. S. E. Asch, "Opinions and Social Pressure," *Scientific American* 193 (1955): 33–35.
2. M. Sherif, "A Study of Some Social Factors in Perception," *Archives of Psychology*, 27 (1935): 187.
3. I. L. Janis, *Victims of Groupthink*, (Boston: Houghton Mifflin, 1972):197–204.
4. R. Rose, *12 Angry Men*. Released 29 July 1957, Orion-Nova Productions.
5. D. Ostle, "The Culture Clash at DaimlerChrysler was Worse than Expected," *Automotive News Europe*, vol. 4, issue 24 (1999): 3.
6. D. G. Myers and S. J. Arenson, "Enhancement of Dominant Risk Tendencies in Group Discussion," *Psychological Reports* 30 (1972): 615–623.
7. R. B. Zajonc, A. Heingartner, and E. M. Herman, "Social Enhancement and Impairment of Performance in the Cockroach," *Journal of Personality and Social Psychology*, 13 (1969): 83–92.
8. G. Marwell and D. R. Schmitt, "Dimensions of Compliance-Gaining Behavior: An Empirical Analysis," *Sociometry* 30 (1967): 350–364.
9. R. B. Cialdini, *Influence: Science and Practice,* 4th ed. (Boston: Allyn and Bacon, 2001).
10. P. R. Kunz and M. Woolcott, "Season's Greetings: From my Status to Yours," *Social Science Research,* 5 (1976): 269–278.
11. Cialdini, 100.
12. C. K. Hofling, E. Brotzman, and S. Dalrymple, "An Experimental Study in Nurse-Physician Relationships" *Journal of Nervous and Mental Disease* 143 (1966): 171–180.
13. R. Levine, *The Power of Persuasion*: *How We're Bought and Sold,* (Hoboken, New Jersey: John Wiley & Sons, 2003):29–64.
14. S. Milgram, *Obedience to Authority*: *An Experimental View* (New York: Harper & Row, 1974).
15. Ibid., 18.
16. E. Tarnow, "Toward the Zero Accident Goal: Assisting the First Officer Monitor and Challenge Captain Errors," *Journal of Aviation/Aerospace Education and Research* 10, 1 (2000).

CHAPTER

3 TRUE PERSUASION: CHANGING MINDS

In this book, we draw a distinction between what we might call true persuasion and other forms of social influence. There is a pragmatic reason for a manager to make that distinction. True persuasion, as we are using the expression, means that a change in response to influence is internalized, that there is "buy-in" among the recipients. This means that the result of the influential message won't be limited to a temporary change in behavior and only in behavior that is observed.

Managers don't always need to create this sort of change, but it is nearly always preferable. In some cases, it offers obvious and critical advantages. When a leader communicates his vision, when a team pitches its strategy, when a manager wants to change organizational culture, a surface-level behavioral response is not enough.

Much of the research in persuasion has been done on attitude change. This is due largely to the practicality of studying attitude change rather than behavioral change resulting from internalizing a message. Measuring attitude change in a lab is a fairly straightforward process that can be completed very quickly after exposure to a persuasive message. Waiting to measure a behavioral change, on the other hand, can be a bit tricky. Some clever researchers have found ways to do this, but the majority of them have settled for measures of attitude change.

We will begin our discussion of true persuasion first by discussing what attitudes are, how they are formed and why we have them, and then by examining some of the research on changing attitudes. We'll learn how to craft a persuasive message and explore why a well crafted message may or may not turn out to be persuasive.

ATTITUDE BASICS

According to Martin Fishbein and Icek Ajzen, two popular researchers in this area, *an attitude is a learned predisposition to respond favorably or unfavorably to an attitude object.*[1] Important to note in this definition is the word "learned." We are not born with our attitudes, even though we may have acquired some of our attitudes at a very young age. Also noteworthy is the expression "attitude object." An attitude object can be anything that you can have a thought about. Attitude objects can be people, places, things, ideas, ideologies, events, and more. This definition also suggests that attitudes are all evaluative. Not all researchers would agree with the belief that attitudes must be positive or negative. Some believe people can have neutral attitudes.

Attitudes have three different components: Affect, behavior, and cognition, often referred to as the ABCs of attitudes. *Affect* refers to our emotional reaction to an attitude object, *behavior* is how we tend to behave toward the attitude object, and *cognition* refers to our beliefs about attitude objects. Our attitudes can vary in terms of which part is the most important in driving a particular attitude. For example, what is your attitude toward spiders—especially large, black spiders with fat, furry legs, multiple red eyes, and visible fangs? Many people have a very negative attitude toward spiders and that attitude is driven largely by their emotional or affective response to them. What about your attitude toward toothbrushes? Most people don't get terribly emotional about their toothbrush. They may have a positive attitude toward toothbrushes in general because of the beliefs they have about their value and their regular use of a toothbrush, so their attitude is primarily driven by the cognitive and behavioral components.

One interesting question about the components of attitudes is "which comes first?" How are attitudes formed? Intuitively, it seems as though we would develop a set of beliefs about an attitude object and then base our attitude on those beliefs, but think about spiders again. We can have a very negative attitude about spiders without knowing much about them. Research shows that attitudes can be formed almost immediately, based on an affective response. Consider, for example a person you meet and take an immediate liking to. Or perhaps, someone you meet and dislike right away. You don't need to know anything about that person to form your attitude; you just have a feeling about him or her.

But what about behavior? Can behavior toward an attitude object precede our attitude? Can we develop an attitude based on our behavior? And could our behavior ever inform our attitude? As counterintuitive as this may sound, research shows that sometimes we do look to our own behavior to determine our attitude and not the other way around. Self-perception theory states that we observe our own behavior and infer our attitudes from the observation.[2] People expert in the art of social influence are well aware of this process. An Arizona-based religious cult asks visitors who are thinking of becoming new members to write essays about the leader and his teaching. The essays are then read by the leader, so they are most likely positive commentaries. Having people spend time writing down complimentary

---

Different Attitude Functions can Drive Attitudes Toward a Single Object

When the Haulopi Indian tribe opened the Grand Canyon Skywalk in Arizona, it was to mixed reviews. The tribe expects the Skywalk to be a major tourist attraction generating revenue for their reservation. However, others outside the tribe believe the structure defaces the canyon. Even within the tribe, some people feel that the responsibility of the tribe to be good stewards of the canyon are being sacrificed for commercialism and view the skywalk as a desecration of a sacred place. Still others have a very different view of the skywalk. With the glass-bottom walkway extending 70 feet from the rim of the canyon and hovering 4,000 feet above the canyon floor, the whole idea of the bridge makes some people a little nervous. What attitude functions do you think are being served by these varying attitudes?

Figure 3.1   The skywalk over the Grand Canyon

things about you of their free will can do wonders for their attitude toward you. For the group in Arizona, this occurs shortly before converts are asked to sign over all of their possessions.

Our attitudes do not remain static once they are formed. Consider the example of the person you immediately dislike. You may learn more about that person over time and come to like him or her very much. Attitudes can change, and that change may be due to new information, whether affective or cognitive, or observations of your own behavior.

Persuaders often recognize that attitudes are driven by different components and, with some attitude objects, it is easy to predict whether an attitude will be largely affective, cognitive, or behavioral. For example, your attitude toward dessert items on a menu is probably based on an affective response. Pictures and descriptive words will be more powerful messages than long paragraphs of text about the ingredients and how a dessert was made. Your decision to purchase a new refrigerator might be based more on beliefs about the product, and you would expect a salesperson to tell you key information about the unit's capacity, energy rating, and cost.

Another important question about attitudes is "why do we have them?" The functional theory of attitudes suggests that we hold attitudes to help us reach our goals and protect us from harm. A number of specific functions are served by the various attitudes we hold:[3, 4]

- **Knowledge function.** The knowledge function is served by attitudes we hold that help us navigate our way successfully through the world. The emphasis is on the need to be informed and the need for order, structure, and meaning. We like the Weather Channel because it helps us plan our week.
- **Utilitarian function.** Closely related is the utilitarian function, which emphasizes maximizing rewards or benefits and minimizing costs. We hold attitudes serving this function toward objects that generally serve some sort of purpose for us. We like our vacuum cleaner because it works great and was a good value.
  - **Social-adjustive function.** Attitudes that serve a social-adjustive function help us initiate, maintain, or terminate relationships. We like the same fashions as the cool kids, and don't like the brand of jeans that the nerds wear.
  - **Value-expressive function.** The value-expressive function is served by attitudes that help us express our values. We like hybrid cars because being good stewards of the planet is important to us.
  - **Ego-defensive function.** The ego-defensive function is served by attitudes that protect us from harm or embarrassment or preserve our self-image. Often the true reasons behind these attitudes operate at a level below our conscious awareness.

The functional approach to attitudes suggests that if you want to change the attitude of another, you must first understand the function served by that attitude and then target that function with your message. Take for example the challenge facing the World Health Organization (WHO) in remote villages in India where there is resurgence of polio. The WHO transports vaccine to these villages and meets with resistance from parents who don't want their children vaccinated. Sometimes the villagers have heard stories, false rumors, from other villages about children dying from the vaccine, so they are afraid. In other cases, they are concerned about offending Allah by not trusting him to keep their children safe. These attitudes are not going to be changed by medical workers who come into the village armed with statistics about disease prevalence and contagiousness. They need to make a different argument, perhaps through the local religious leaders.

Attitudes toward any given attitude object can serve more than one function, and clever marketers recognize this and are taking advantage of it. The (RED) campaign is a good example. This campaign features red items, (e.g., a red Motorola Razr cell phone, red message Ts from the Gap, a red Apple iPod) for sale from different retailers where a portion of the proceeds from each sale goes to The Global Fund which helps combat AIDS in Africa. What function is being served by attitudes toward these items? It could be one of many. Ordinarily you might expect an attitude toward a cell phone to be utilitarian, but it could be value-expressive with the (RED) phone. On the other hand, the function could be social-adjustive if it's considered cool to support the campaign and you get to whip out your (RED) phone in front of your friends.

Of course, offering consumers more than one reason for an attitude about a product has been going on for a long time. In elementary school, when kids enter the lunchroom with their TMNT lunchbox (teenage mutant ninja turtles, for those of you who don't know), that box is more than just a container to carry some food. Pity the child who has just a plain brown bag. A positive attitude toward a TMNT lunchbox might serve a social-adjustive function for a boy trying to fit in with his peers, and a negative attitude toward a plain brown bag might be serve an ego-defensive function for a fourth grader who doesn't want to feel embarrassed.

DO ATTITUDES PREDICT BEHAVIOR?

In the early days of attitude research, it was simply assumed that one's behavior would generally correspond to one's attitudes. Then in 1934, a man named Richard LaPiere conducted an interesting study that shook that assumption to its foundation. LaPiere, a sociologist, had been traveling in the United States with a Chinese couple, and he was surprised at how well the couple was received at a nice hotel in a small town. This surprised him, because in the 1930's the United States was far from embracing ethnic diversity. Catholics, the Irish, Jews, Blacks and others were the objects of blatant discrimination that was considered an acceptable part to the culture. Most upscale establishments at that time would have openly discriminated against the Chinese couple.

LaPiere was so surprised by the way his traveling companions were treated that he contacted the same establishment later and asked if they would be willing to accommodate an "important Chinese gentleman." He was promptly told, "No."

This gave LaPiere the idea for his study. He traveled around the United States with the Chinese couple and observed the behavior of hotel clerks, waiters and waitresses, bellhops, and others. In all, they visited 251 establishments. Of those, only one refused to serve them. Six months after visiting, LaPiere sent the establishments a letter asking if they would be willing to "accommodate an important Chinese gentleman." About half of the establishments responded to the letter. Of those responses, over 90% replied that they would not allow Chinese people in their establishment.[5]

This study was the first systematic attempt to investigate the correspondence between attitudes and behavior and, thus, first to show the correspondence to be nearly nil. Does this mean that there is no point in studying attitudes because they have nothing to do with behavior? Not exactly. LaPiere's study had quite a few flaws. He only received responses to half the letters. The people responding to the letters were probably not the same people who served the couple when they visited. The people responding to the letter were probably just giving a response based on policy, which might not reflect their personal attitude at all. So, the study is hardly perfect and should not lead us to conclude there is no correspondence between attitudes and behavior. Nevertheless, LaPiere was the first to study this issue and deserves credit for bringing attention to it. This study began the ongoing effort to better understand the relationship between attitudes and behavior.

So, what is the correspondence? Attitudes do a good job of predicting behavior in some cases, and not in others. General attitudes don't do a very good job of predicting specific behaviors. For example, if you were asked about your attitude toward making donations toward worthy causes, you might indicate a favorable attitude. But if someone called later this week and asked you to donate money to a charity over the phone, you might refuse. Does that mean your attitudes don't predict your behaviors? Maybe what it really means it that you have a rule against donating money over the phone. Or perhaps you have a group of organizations you give faithfully to and don't have money left to give to others. The problem isn't really a lack of correspondence between attitudes and behavior but rather a lack of correspondence between the type of question being asked and the type of behavior being observed. The question is about a very general attitude, but the behavior is very specific. If the question asked was about your attitude toward donating to Charity XYZ over the telephone, your reported attitude would be much more likely to correspond to your behavior. Questions about general attitudes need to allow for multiple behavioral options for correspondence to be present.

Situational factors can lead someone to act in way that is inconsistent with their attitudes. Let's say that you indicate a favorable attitude to the question above about donating money over the phone to XYZ, but you are a student without extra money, so you can't really afford to donate later in the week if you get a donation request.

Some factors increase the probability that attitudes will predict behaviors. Stronger attitudes or attitudes that are central to one's belief system are more likely to predict behavior. For example, if you strongly support a flat tax rate, have always supported a flat tax rate, and consider it one of your pet issues, you are likely to engage in behaviors that show your support for a flat tax rate and that behavior will be more predictable. Accessibility of an attitude is also more likely to predict behavior. If someone is reminded of an attitude right before exposure to an opportunity to act on it, they are more likely to act according to their attitude.

Personality is yet another factor that contributes to whether attitudes will predict behavior. A personality trait called "self-monitoring" is a popular individual difference variable for researchers in marketing, attitudes, and persuasion. Self-monitoring refers to the tendency of individuals to pay attention to and use social cues in their environment to modify their behavior for social appropriateness. People who are high in self monitoring are more likely to behave in ways that respond to social cues, whereas people low in self-monitoring are more likely to respond to internal cues, such as attitudes or values. The behavior of low self-monitors is more likely to reflect attitudes.[6]

A crucial point to remember about attitudes with respect to behavior is that behavior is not solely the result of an attitude. Attitudes contribute to behavior, but they are not the single cause. The "theory of planned behavior" does a nice job of finding a home for attitudes in the prediction of behavior without giving them too much weight, nor dismissing their importance.[7]

As you can see from the diagram in Figure 3.2, the theory of planned behavior suggests that behavior is the result of our intention to behave in a certain way. Our intentions, in turn, are formed from a combination of our attitude toward a behavior and the subjective norm about that behavior, or what other people who are important to us think about the behavior. The terms used in the theory of planned behavior are defined in the following bullet points:

- **Behavioral beliefs.** These are our subjective beliefs about the probability that the behavior will produce certain outcomes.
- **Attitude toward the behavior.** This is the degree to which the behavior is positively or negatively valued.

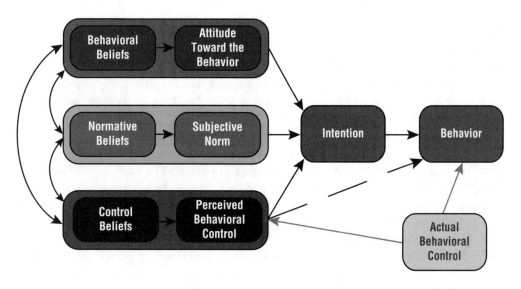

Figure 3.2

Source: http://www.people.umass.edu/aizen/tpb.diag.html

- **Normative beliefs.** These are the beliefs we have about the expectations of other individuals or group who are important to us.
- **Subjective norms.** This is the expected social pressure to engage or not engage in a behavior.
- **Control beliefs.** These are our beliefs about the presence of factors that may help or hinder us in performing a behavior.
- **Perceived behavioral control.** This is our perception of our ability to perform a behavior.
- **Intention.** This is our readiness to perform a behavior and is the direct antecedent to the behavior.
- **Actual behavioral control.** This refers to our possession of the skills and resources required to complete the behavior.

Intention, then, results from our attitude toward the behavior, subjective norms, and perceived behavioral control. Our intentions may not lead to behavior when something beyond our control interferes. Consider this example: Suppose after living in an apartment in the city for a few years, you begin to contemplate buying a house in the suburbs.

- **Attitude toward the behavior.** *I believe buying a house will be beneficial. I will have more room, and it will be a good investment.*
- **Subjective norms.** *My family wants me to buy a house.*
- **Perceived behavioral control.** I am able to secure financing.
- **Intention.** I plan to buy a house.
- **Actual behavioral control.** Nothing is preventing me from buying a house in the suburbs.

The likely outcome here would be your purchase of a house in the suburbs. However, even if you have a favorable attitude toward buying a house, you may not actually buy one if any of the other contributors to the behavior worked against taking that action:

- **Attitude toward the behavior.** *I believe buying a house will be beneficial. I will have more room and it will be a good investment.*
- **Subjective norms.** *My spouse will leave me if we move out of the city.*
- **Perceived behavioral control.** My credit is in bad shape right now and I might not be able to get a loan.
- **Actual behavioral control.** No houses in my price range are on the market in the right area at this time.

CAN ATTITUDES BE CHANGED?

We've already said that attitudes can be changed. It's helpful to understand as much as we can about how and when this happens, and under what circumstances. In general, attitude change can result from one of two mental processes: *Central route processing* or *peripheral route processing*. The word "processing" refers to how much mental or cognitive energy is expended in processing a message. Everyone does both types of processing, but people vary in terms of how often they do each and under what circumstances.

If you are processing via the central route, you are doing deep thinking about the message. You are weighing it against what you currently believe, checking it against your own experience, and generating issue-relevant thoughts. In contrast, if you are doing peripheral route processing, you are deciding how to respond to the message while doing as little cognitive work as possible. To make a decision using the peripheral route, you will look for cues in the environment to help you determine how to respond to a persuasive message. For example, if you and several colleagues listen to a presentation, you might observe how your colleagues are responding and use their response as a cue to guide your own. If your colleagues are smiling and nodding "yes" in agreement, you might respond favorably to the message. If you are receiving a persuasive message from a trusted source whose opinion you typically agree with, you might use the source of the message as a cue.

You can think of these two different processing routes as the end points of an elaboration or depth of processing continuum. This dual processing theory is called the Elaboration Likelihood Model (ELM), and it suggests that people are motivated to hold correct or beneficial attitudes, but they would generally like to reach those attitudes with as little cognitive effort as possible.[8]

So when do we choose the peripheral route and when do we choose the central route for processing messages? Many researchers argue that people, in general, are cognitive misers in that, if they can get away with using less cognitive capacity, they would prefer that, making peripheral route processing the default. This is probably not true for everyone, however, since some people are very high in what is called "need for cognition." People high in the need for cognition really enjoy doing a lot of heavy mental lifting and will likely default to more central route processing.

In order to do central route processing, you must have two things: Ability and motivation. Lack of ability doesn't mean a lack of intelligence. Many factors can compromise one's ability to process deeply. One example, distractions. How deeply can you think about a message if you are trying to do something else at the same time? Other factors, such as a language barrier, lack of appropriate knowledge structures, time constraints, or fatigue can compromise a person's ability. Motivation is necessary to in order for people to expend the effort required to think deeply. Motivation usually comes from some personal involvement in an issue. If a message has nothing to do with you, you probably won't be motivated to pay particular attention to it.

Some important points should be made about the ELM. First, central route processing does not mean that persuasion will occur. Think about a time when you were listening to an argument and, through thinking deeply about it, you recognized the flaws in the logic and poor quality of the evidence presented. In those moments, you were engaged in central route processing, but you were basically thinking of reasons why you should not be persuaded. This could, in fact, move you even further away from the argued position, because you are producing counterarguments.

Second, central route processing is not necessarily objective. You can do deep-level, biased processing. Let's say for example you are listening to an argument made by a source for whom you have low regard. You may listen deeply to the argument and pay especially close attention to anything you think makes the argument weaker. The reverse is also true: You may process the message from a well-liked source with a favorable bias.

Variables associated with a message can affect how it is processed in several ways: It can serve as an argument, it can serve as a peripheral cue, or it can lead a person to process a message more or less deeply. A variable is anything that can vary, so it's a very broad statement. Let's consider an example. Suppose we are choosing the face to appear in a print ad for our anti-wrinkle cream. We can choose from literally thousands of beautiful models, so since the face can vary, the face is a variable. We decide to use a beautiful, very successful, well-liked, seasoned model. How can this variable affect processing?

- Can this variable serve as an argument? Yes, in a few ways. If we believe (naively) that the photo of the face in the ad has not been retouched and this model is an older model, but still has no visible wrinkles, we may view the face as evidence the product works. We might also view this face as an argument if we know that this model has had a long and successful career. We may think she can afford to be selective about the products she endorses, and if she chose this one, it must be good. After all, with her experience, she is likely to have a certain level of expertise in beauty products.
- Could this variable serve as a peripheral cue? Certainly. She's beautiful. She's well liked. The picture in the ad is likely to show few if any wrinkles in her skin.
- Could her presence in the ad make you think about the message more or less deeply? Yes, in a number of different ways. Fans of this model may simply use her as a peripheral cue and not process deeply. On the other hand, fans who respect this model may motivated by her presence in the ad to think more deeply about the product and read the text in the ad.

What would happen if you decided to go a different way, to use the fresh new face of a younger model for the ad? The beauty of the model could serve as a persuasive peripheral cue. On the other hand, the youth of the model might serve as a cue too, not one that would work in our favor. The younger model might lead people to dismiss our ad and not process it deeply since she obviously isn't old enough to use the product and know its effectiveness.

Peripheral cues become more important as the ability or motivation to process goes down. For example, let's say you have a very credible source for a message, perhaps the trusted and admired CEO of your company. If people are unable to process the message because of some distraction, say the audio equipment is acting up, the credibility cue could still lead to persuasion. On the other hand, to the extent that people are motivated and able to process a message deeply, the source becomes less important than the merits of the argument. A credible source making a really lousy argument to a centrally processing audience is not going to be very effective.

So if you are attempting to persuade someone, what it the best method to use? Should you make a good argument or provide a peripheral cue? Well, that's an important question because, even though both routes can lead to persuasion, the resulting persuasion is qualitatively different depending on the route of processing. Attitude change that results from central route processing is more enduring, more likely to predict behavior, and more resistant to counterarguments. This makes sense when you think about it. People have thought things through when they are persuaded by central route processing. They've reasoned things out. They know *what* they believe, but they also know *why* they believe what they do. If you can make a strong argument, and you can motivate your audience to process it, there are some definite advantages.

Of course, it never hurts to have a good peripheral cue as a back-up and numerous cues are available. Characteristics of the source of the persuasive message, such as attractiveness, similarity, expertise, and overall perceived credibility can each be a peripheral cue. The response of other people receiving the message can provide a cue of social proof. The mood you are in can be a peripheral cue. If a message makes you feel good, that might be all you need to know.

Even familiarity can be a peripheral cue. Research shows that "mere exposure" or just being exposed to something we are neutral about, can lead us to have a more favorable response toward that stimulus later.[9] This holds true only to a point. Too much repetition can work against you: Seeing a commercial you are sick of a few more times is not going to have a positive effect on your attitude. Similarly, repeated exposure to something you don't like can have the opposite effect and can actually lead to a more negative attitude. The key here is to repeat enough to create some recognition, but not enough to tire people of your message. A marketing research project for a personal injury law firm illustrated this effect. Firms that advertised occasionally on T.V. and had recognizable names were rated most favorably; firms that didn't advertise on T.V. at all were not rated highly; and the firm that advertised on T.V., billboards, posters in the mall, and full page covers on the back of the phone book was rated the lowest. Comments about the latter firm indicated people were tired of seeing advertisements for that firm everywhere they looked.

CREATING YOUR MESSAGE: BUILDING A STRONG ARGUMENT

How do you create a strong argument that people will believe and will be motivated to process? To answer this question we can go back in history well before the first psychological study of attitude change was conceived, all the way to Aristotle. He described three different means of persuasion: Logos, pathos, and ethos. *Logos* is an appeal based on logic, *pathos* is an appeal based on emotion, and *ethos* is an appeal based on the credibility of the speaker or source of the message. People haven't changed much since Aristotle's day when it comes to persuasion. Even after all these years, people are still affected by good arguments, emotional appeals, and a credible source. If you are able to present all three in a persuasive effort, you increase your chances for success. As we have already seen, not all three are necessary.

We'll begin our discussion of these three elements with logos. One common way to talk about argumentation is to start with a proposition. A proposition is simply a statement that can be argued, and propositions can make several different kinds of statements:

■ **A proposition of fact** states that something is or isn't, was or wasn't, will or won't be, or that one thing causes another. They are not fact, but rather statements of belief that need to be supported with evidence. It is a proposed fact and, as such, can be argued.

Example: *In twenty years, newspapers will be a thing of the past.*

■ **A proposition of value** is an evaluative judgment and argues that something is good or bad, moral or immoral, right or wrong.

Example: *Rupert Murdock's purchase of The Wall Street Journal will be good for the paper.*

■ **A proposition of policy** is an argument for action. It states that something should or should not be done.

Example: *Newspapers should focus their attention on increasing their online readership.*

For each type of proposition, certain stock issues must be addressed to create a solid argument. With propositions of value and sometimes propositions of fact, the stock issues are typically the definitive and designative issues. Definitive issues involve creating and agreeing upon the meaning of words in the proposition, and designative issues involve proving that the conditions laid out in the definitive issues are met. For example, consider the proposition "Our product XYZ is obsolete." To make that argument, everyone would first need to agree on what "obsolete" means, and then see if the conditions stated in the definition are met with respect to product XYZ. This example sounds easy enough, but consider a proposition of value, such as "Targeting children with advertisements for unhealthy treats is wrong." Making this argument means getting everyone to agree on what it means to target children with an ad and what constitutes an unhealthy treat, as well as agreeing on the definition of "wrong." Agreeing on a standard for evaluative words like "wrong" or "good" can make values arguments very difficult.

Causal arguments are also some of the most challenging to construct. In order to argue causality, you must be able to show correspondence between the cause and the effect, temporal precedence (the cause came before the effect), and the elimination of other possible causes. Meeting these conditions can be very difficult, outside of a laboratory experiment, although it can be done. Recently a morning new program reported that plastic surgeries had increased 7% since the beginning of reality television makeover shows like *The Swan* and *Extreme Makeover*. They attributed the increase to the airing of these shows. However, another news program recently reported the increase in the plastic surgeries but attributed it to the rise in the number of men having procedures. Neither report established temporal precedence; in other words, neither one talked about the rate of increase in plastic surgeries in years past to show that the number of procedures wasn't already on the rise. And neither made an effort to show the elimination of other causes. Building a causal argument without research findings from controlled experiments requires using many kinds of evidence.

The stock issues for *propositions of policy* include the demonstration of need for action. You have to show something is broken before you can ask people to fix it. The action proposed must be shown to meet the need or solve the problem, it must be practical or doable, and the benefits must outweigh the risks. For example, you might argue that your company should buy catfish farmed in the United States instead of importing it from southern China. If the problem you are solving is not well known, you must show it exists. Perhaps your customers are refusing fish imported from China. The action must solve the problem in a way that is practical and doable. What is the difference in cost? Is there enough U.S. farm-raised catfish available to meet your needs? Will the increased sales outweigh the costs?

In the language of argumentation, an *assertion* is just a statement of a proposition. A *claim* is an assertion supported by evidence. And a *warrant i*s the usually unspoken, culturally shared belief that connects the evidence to the claim. For example, if someone said, "Well, both the candidates have the qualifications to be promoted to management, but Beth doesn't like to travel, so I think Rachel is a better choice." The shared assumption is that the management promotion requires travel. The evidence "Beth doesn't like to travel" wouldn't make sense if this assumption wasn't understood by the listener.

The warrant is usually not stated, but don't think that means it doesn't matter. If you accept the argument, you are accepting the warrant. So the warrant is worth examining. What if the evidence offered were something like, "Beth doesn't like to play golf, so I think Rachel is a better choice." The assumption that the promotion to management requires golfing skills might not be one the listener agrees with.

Sometimes qualifications are used to make the claim more precise and set conditions for when the evidence supports it or when the claim is true, for example, "Opening a new store in Collegetown would increase our annual sales if we are able to find a suitable location within one mile of the college campus," and "We should require candidates for the new position to have an MBA if they don't have much work experience."

Whether you are crafting an argument or are on the receiving end of one, analyzing the evidence offered is essential. Not all evidence is created equal. Evidence offered for support should be carefully evaluated for quality. Furthermore, most arguments will require more than one piece of evidence. Evidence should be relevant, precise, accurate, sufficient, representative, authoritative, and clearly expressed.[10]

Let's look at each of these in turn with an example. An area nonprofit organization provides housing for male ex-convicts convicted of nonviolent crimes. The mission of the organization is to help the men re-enter society and, as part of this effort, they try to help the men find jobs. The staff of the organization calls potential employers and pitches their residents. As you can imagine, this is often a hard sell. Some of the evidence the staffers can offer in support of a claim that their residents would be good employees include the following:

- Committed only nonviolent crimes
- Are motivated to do well
- Need a break
- Have social support
- Have a curfew
- Are drug tested
- Overall, residents have history of few absences, tardies, and no-shows after securing employment.

Is the evidence relevant? Some employers might not consider the fact that the men need a break to be relevant evidence of their ability to be a good employee. Some employers might interpret that as relevant, though, expecting it will mean lower turnover with the men.

Is the evidence precise? It is not precise as it's written and could be more effective if it were more precise. For example, how often are the residents drug tested? What is their curfew and does that mean they can't work at night? What are the statistics on longevity of employment for residents in the past? What sort of social support is offered? Do they have a ride to work?

Is the evidence accurate? For consumers of a persuasive message, accuracy can be difficult to judge in the moment. Independent research might be required to confirm the accuracy of a claim, and every so often, only time will tell. The evidence offered by the nonprofit can be assumed to accurate to the extent that the organization has access to the accurate information. They may know, for example, what crime a resident was convicted of, but might not really know how motivated the resident is.

Is the evidence sufficient? No piece of evidence by itself is sufficient. For example, needing a break isn't enough. It's safe to assume most people looking for a job need one, so that's not a good enough reason to hire someone. Is it sufficient that a crime was nonviolent? What if the crime was a nonviolent robbery, and the job opening involves operating a cash register? Taken together, however, the evidence might be convincing.

Is the evidence representative? If the organization has a long history with a good number of success stories, then the evidence could be considered representative. To better judge representativeness, it would be useful to know how many residents there have been and what percentage of them have been successful at returning to work.

Is the evidence authoritative? Is this evidence presented by someone who would be an authority? The organization is very small, and the staff interacts regularly with the residents, so it's fair to assume that they would know the men well enough to be an authoritative source. Note, however, that if employers are not aware that the staffers have personal contact with the residents, the staff may not be perceived as authoritative, so that contact should be made known.

Is the evidence clearly expressed? The evidence offered by the organization is straightforward and clear. If they were to increase the precision of their evidence by adding some statistics, they would want to be careful to make them easy to understand.

FRAMING MESSAGES

Frames represent the perspective from which something will be viewed. The process contributes to the meanings individuals assign to messages. Through the framing of messages, the packaging of messages will tend to emphasize one interpretation and downplay another. Creating frames and changing frames is like changing the gels on stage lights: The set is still the same, but the look and feel can be fantastically altered when cast in a different light.

Frames can be created through a single word. All *natural* frames granola bars as health food. *Luxury* or *deluxe* frames an item as special and or better quality. *Fat Free* frames a food as a diet food. Tax *relief* frames a tax program as a relief from burden. Frames can be changed when people are given a new way to view something. For example, under-the-sink water purifiers can be thought of as an affordable way to improve your drinking water. This thinking might not motivate you to install a water purifier, however, because so many other, perhaps more convenient, options for purified water exist, such as bottled water. If someone wanted to change your frame for thinking about water purifiers, they could begin by telling you about the damage caused to the environment by bottled water, "Plastic water bottles are flooding our landfills. We throw away about 38 billion water bottles a year." But your thinking about water purifiers might change if they are framed as investments in the environment.

Metaphors can create frames. Metaphors can be used to stimulate new thought and help us see things in a new way. How would we approach the board of directors if we view them as a brick wall? How would we run our company if we saw it as a symphony orchestra? How would we design small appliances if we thought of them as art? What if challenges could be framed as contests, competitors as romantic rivals, a tough time as a dance marathon?

Framing goals can be a key strategic move for the persuader. Consider the story of the three bricklayers. A man came along and asked the first bricklayer what he was doing, and he replied "I'm laying these bricks." The man went to the second bricklayer and asked him the same question. "I'm building a wall," was the reply. The man went to the third bricklayer and asked him what he was doing and the bricklayer said, "I'm building a cathedral." The bricklayers were viewing the same task through different frames. If we were employing the three bricklayers, we would probably like them to all have the perspective of the third. He framed his work in a way that will guide his actions toward a goal larger than the immediate task. Goals should be framed in a way that identifies common ground between the persuader and the recipient. And remember, goals don't have to be something tangible. A goal could be holding the correct belief (who wants to be thought of as "wrong?") or fitting in with a desirable group.

Framing a message may involve a pre-message communication. You may for example, send a memo or letter, or give a presentation that prepares the audience for the forthcoming message. Say, for example, you wholeheartedly believe that your organization will be faced with a sell-off without significant changes. The changes you believe are needed include splitting the company into two divisions, a major reorganization, and relocation for some key employees. Most employees would be unhappy about these changes, but framing this message as a way to prevent a sale might make these recommendations more palatable. Before you can frame the message in that way, however, you need to let the employees know that a the threat of sale exists. You could inform them of this unfortunate reality with a message delivered before your main communication.

Frames can also be meta-communicational. In other words, communicate about the communication. For example, a message might be prefaced with the meta-communicational statement, "This is going to sound like a wild and crazy idea but . . . " Meta-communication can be a way of breaking a frame that we feel ourselves being pulled into. Perhaps if we are being cast as the villain in a company meeting, we may break the frame by becoming meta-communicational and asking the person about their communication—what are they trying to say or what are they trying to imply. One caveat: This is not always going to be an appropriate way to defend yourself, especially if the other person is trying to cast you as paranoid and defensive. The point is that you can, as an agent of influence, interrupt the frame of another agent of influence with whom you do not agree.

In his book, *The Power of Persuasion: How We're Bought and Sold*, Robert Levine offers a list of helpful suggestions for effective framing when we are faced with framing losses and gains.[11]

1. **People are more interested in avoiding pain than in acquiring a reward.** People will try harder to escape bad feelings than they will to achieve good feelings. People are also more willing to take a risk to try to prevent bad feelings. For example, which would you prefer: To lose money every month on your energy bill because of energy inefficiency in your home or to save money every month on your energy bill by improving the energy efficiency of your home?

2. **If a small gain accompanies a large loss, then the gain isn't really noticed and the benefit is lost.** To bring attention to savings, the local supermarket tells customers how much they've saved every time they shop with them and use their shopping card when they check out. The checker will also circle the amount of savings in red, which is printed at the bottom of the receipt.

3. **Several small losses are harder to take than one big loss.** People respond better to a large loss than to many small losses. Let's say you are charged with reducing the costs of perks enjoyed by your employees. You have to tell them that their gym membership will no longer be paid for by the company, the free bagels have seen their last sunrise in your break room, and the masseuse with the portable massage chair won't be coming back. You might think breaking the news to them slowly: The bagels one day, the gym the next, etc. would be the best way to go, but Levine says no. It will go down easier in one big gulp.

4. **Bundle small losses into larger gains.** In many organizations, United Way donations come right out of employees' paychecks. The donation seems small, relative to the gain of the paycheck.

5. **List high, sell low.** This provides the contract effect we've mentioned before. It's a tactic used by furniture stores for example. A sofa might be marked $1799, but it's on sale for $899. The store would be thrilled for someone to pay $1799, but their actual goal for markup is the $899 price.

OTHER MESSAGE FACTORS

A well-organized message with quality evidence citing credible sources is a great start, but a few other questions are often asked by persuaders attempting to construct a truly influential message.

Should the conclusion drawn from your argument be explicit or implicit? In other words, should you state your conclusion outright, or should you let your audience digest the argument you've made and reach *your* conclusion on their own. If the audience is able to reach the conclusion you're hoping for without you spelling it out for them, the resulting persuasion will be stronger. The "Get a Mac" campaign from Apple is a good example of the implicit message. Through a series of commercial ads, we meet two young men. The laid back, cool, hip looking guy with all the confidence, for whom everything seems to work well is the Mac, and the unfortunate looking fellow wearing glasses and cubicle-bound suit, for whom everything seems to be a problem, is, of course, the PC. The message is clear, even though it isn't actually stated in the ad: Get a Mac. On the other hand, if you don't state your conclusion, the conclusion the audience comes to might be different from the one you intended. If there is little chance for confusion, then it is best to let the audience generate the conclusion. However, if you are not certain they are able to reach the right conclusion on their own, you should play it safe and state the conclusion for them.

Should I be direct in my language? Use an assertive style of speech rather than powerless speech. Powerless speech uses confirming questions, fillers, qualifiers, and negative preambles. It weakens the argument being made, should be avoided, and can compromise the perceived competence of the persuader.

For example, instead of saying: "In my opinion, Proposal B is the best one, don't you think? I really think it was the best because . . . uhm . . . of the savings, right? And also because of the . . . uhm . . . tax advantages."

Say: "Proposal B offers a substantial savings and a significant tax advantage, which clearly makes it the best choice."

Of course, sometimes the use of powerless language can be employed by someone who might otherwise seem threatening, to create the "regular folk" effect.

If my position is extreme, should my message be extreme? *Social judgment theory* says that you should consider the position of your target audience, and then position your argument so it is a small move in the desired direction for your audience. For any topic, a range of positions is possible. For example, consider the positions below for red wine consumption:

1. Red wine, and all other alcohol, is evil and should be abolished completely.
2. Consumption of red wine should be highly regulated and only permitted in limited quantities for religious rituals.
3. Consumption of red wine produces problems for society and should be discouraged.
4. The state should regulate consumption of red wine to people 21 and over.
5. Red wine has health benefits and should be consumed often by people 21 and over.
6. Red wine has health benefits, and daily consumption by adults should be encouraged.
7. People of all ages should be encouraged to consume red wine regularly.
8. Children should be taught the benefits of drinking red wine and be made to drink it with their meals.

On this continuum of positions, we will all have a preferred point, called an *anchor*. The anchor is the preferred position, but not necessarily the only position acceptable. For example, you might think that the state should regulate the consumption of wine to people 21 and over (position 4) and you might also think that the health benefits make it a good idea to consume red wine frequently (position 5). The anchor and the other positions you would find acceptable comprise your *latitude of acceptance*. Two other latitudes that exist outside the latitude of acceptance are defined by social judgment theory: The *latitude of non-commitment and the latitude of rejection.* The latitude of non-commitment represents the positions that the person feels ambivalent about. For example, you may not necessarily support position 6, but you don't oppose it either. The latitude of rejection represents the positions that are considered objectionable. People tend to judge other positions against their anchor point, and if too much discrepancy is discerned between a position being argued and the anchor, the recipient will dismiss it. On the other hand, a message that falls a little closer to the anchor, say in the latitude of non-commitment, is more likely to be perceived as close to the anchor position and is more likely to be accepted. The lesson here is this: Don't argue something that is too far from the audience's original position, or at least, if you do, be prepared for a tougher sell. Social judgment theory also suggests that small increments of persuasion over time could eventually lead to the large change you are looking for.[12]

What is more important, quantity or quality of the argument? Well, it depends. If your audience is processing centrally, then the quality of the arguments is much more important than quantity. In fact, if you are tempted to throw in a few weak or marginal arguments, just so it seems like you have more evidence, don't. You can actually be working against yourself by doing so. When people are centrally processing a message, they are carefully scrutinizing the message and weighing the quality of the evidence presented. Weak arguments can get them thinking about why the argument is flawed and generating counterarguments to refute it. On the other hand, if the audience is processing peripherally, then the quality of the arguments has little impact. The number of arguments, however, can serve as a peripheral cue. So, if you expect your audience to be processing peripherally, more is better.

Should I give both sides of an argument or only the side you support? If your audience will be aware of the arguments for the other side while receiving your message, you are much better off presenting those arguments and refuting them. If you don't, your audience will be producing those counterarguments themselves. If your audience isn't aware of the counterarguments and isn't likely to be exposed to them after receiving your message, then you can give only your side although you should consider the ethics of withholding that information when making this decision. Let's say, for example, you are selling floor coverings and a particular carpet tends to shows significant wear after about five years. If that carpet affords you a slightly higher profit than others you sell, you might be tempted to withhold this information from the customer. They probably won't be aware of it and won't learn about it for some time after their purchase. The answer then rests on the ethical issue. The TARES test would tell us withholding the information would be unethical.

If am making an argument and another person is making the opposite argument to the same audience, should I go first? Again, it depends. In this case, it depends on when the audience will make their decision of which argument to support. If the two arguments will be presented back to back, and then some time will pass before any decision is made, you are better off going first. If, on the other hand there will be a time delay between the two arguments and the decision will be made directly after the second argument is heard, you are better off going second.

Can I do anything to strengthen the endurance of my message against counterarguments my audience may encounter later? Yes, you can inoculate them. This means you can forewarn your audience that others will attempt to persuade them in the future, then give them ways to refute the counterarguments. People tend to become resistant when they are told others are going to attempt to persuade them. For this same reason, it is usually not a good idea to begin your persuasive message by telling the audience, "today I'm going to persuade you . . ." Your audience is likely to respond with a "go ahead and try" attitude.

LOGICAL FALLACIES: THE SLIPPERY SPOT ON THE PATH TO REASON

We often think that people are reasonable, rational beings making carefully considered decisions. In reality, we don't do that nearly as often as we might like to believe. People make decisions without carefully evaluating the merits of an argument all the time and, of course, persuaders know this. We are all vulnerable to the trappings of propaganda and logical fallacies, in part because, at first blush, these arguments seem compelling, but they cannot withstand closer scrutiny. The problem for most of us is that we aren't giving the arguments close scrutiny. Remember, during our discussion of the Elaboration Likelihood Model, we said that people tend to be cognitive misers and close scrutiny requires cognitive effort.

What exactly do we mean by a logical fallacy? A logical fallacy is flawed logic, but it is often not immediately recognizable, meaning an argument can seem compelling even when it has little merit. Several good web sites are available if you are interested in learning about the great number of logical fallacies commonly used. In addition, entire books have been written on the various logical fallacies, most with the objective of teaching people how to recognize them. We will discuss a few of the more common and critical ones for managers to recognize here.

The single cause. When you got dressed this morning, how many factors did you have to consider before deciding what to wear. Perhaps you thought about what the weather would be like, if you had an important meeting scheduled, if you would be seeing a client, or if you had dinner plans immediately after work. You might have also had to consider what you had clean or what your mood dictated for the day. If something important was scheduled, you might have actually tried on more than one shirt or tie to make sure you got just the look you were hoping for. All of these factors go into such a simple decision, and one that you make 365 days a year, assuming you wear some clothing each day. When so much is considered for such a simple decision, does it seem likely that one single factor is the cause of something significant?

Anytime you are given a single cause in an argument for causality, it should be a red flag. The argument may be accurate, but the single cause is so unlikely that any argument based on this claim screams for careful scrutiny. Ask yourself, what else could be going on here? What else could be involved?

Correlation as cause. You may have heard in your statistics class that correlation does not mean causation. Despite everything you may have forgotten from statistics, that statement is one worth remembering. A correlation is simply a linear relationship between two variables. The relationship can be positive, meaning as you go up on one variable, you go up on the other (e.g., education level and starting salary), or negative, meaning as you go up on one variable you go down on the other (e.g., absences and grade in class). Correlations indicate a relationship but are often presented as indication of a causal relationship and this is a misinterpretation.

Consider the example alcohol consumption and grade point average (GPA) of college students. If a college professor surveys students and finds a negative linear relationship between alcohol consumption and GPA, such that as alcohol consumption increases, GPA decreases, how might that correlation be interpreted? It might be very tempting for a college professor, presumably interested in discouraging excessive drinking, to interpret it as increased alcohol consumption causing grades to suffer. But is it equally plausible to interpret the relationship in the other direction? Perhaps students not performing well academically deal with this by consuming more alcohol. In other words, a lower GPA is causing students to drink more. Or perhaps there is another variable causing both the increase in drinking and the lower GPA, and the professor isn't even looking at it. Perhaps it is stress. Higher levels of stress may cause more alcohol consumption and a resulting lower GPA.

There are two problems with inferring causation from correlations. One is directionality. It's a chicken-and-egg problem. We don't know which came first, so we can't determine the direction of the impact. The other is the third variable problem. Since other variables haven't been ruled out, we don't know what role they play.

Establishing causation usually involves controlled experimentation. This is easy enough to design when you are talking about something like establishing the effectiveness of a drug. But many times, we will be dealing with issues that aren't readily examined with a controlled experiment. We then have to rely on our sensible analysis of the data available, and the more data from varied sources the better.

Hasty generalizations. We stated in our discussion of quality evidence that it should be representative. Fallacies of hasty generalization violate this requirement. It is tempting to make a generalization to an entire category after encountering a few examples. For example, if you visit two different car lots and encounter two separate salespeople that seem pushy, you might make the generalization: Car salespeople are pushy. Perhaps this is true, but perhaps not. With all the car salespeople in the world, a sample of two is probably not enough to determine their typical nature.

Sweeping generalizations. Anytime a person uses words like *all, none, always, never*, they should be a red flag to the critical thinker. How often is something *always* true? How many times does *never* really mean never? Absolutes are rarely accurate. They are usually exaggerations and, if an argument includes these sorts of exaggerations, what other imprecision and inaccuracies may it contain?

THE RIGHT MESSAGE FOR THE RIGHT AUDIENCE AT THE RIGHT TIME ...

People will not always respond to a logical argument, no matter how well crafted. You have to know your audience and what's important to them. If a decision is made on price, arguing other terms isn't going to help. Imagine a situation where you have a production line down and need a motor for a machine to get it up and running again. You have several suppliers for the motor, so your Maintenance, Repair, and Operations buyer gets on the phone immediately and calls the suppliers. In this situation, the most important decision-making criterion will be when you can get the part. If one supplier has the part on the shelf and the second has a two-day wait, the decision is easy. The second supplier won't get very far by arguing the advantages of the brand and offering a discount. No single message will be effective with every audience. You can improve your chances for being effective by learning as much as you can about your audience and tailoring your message to meet their needs and expectations. You have to understand what is important to them.

Stating your case in a way that seems to ignore the needs or wants of your audience can create resistance right off the bat because they may not trust you to consider their concerns and, thus, will feel they need to fight for them. They may dig in their heels and see you as an adversary. Part of the process of building credibility and cultivating trust is communicating your interest in the well-being of your audience. Your open-mindedness and willingness to incorporate the audience's needs or wants into your recommendations will help the audience see you as more credible. This means being flexible. You can't be dogmatic and unwilling to yield and, at the same time, be inspirational to your audience. You may have to compromise or change your recommendations a little to meet the audience's needs.

What motivates? It's impossible to list all the specifics, but in general people are motivated by feelings about themselves, feelings others have about them, rewards and punishments, being right and making good decisions, and holding defensible positions. Different motivation will affect how we seek information and what information we attend to. For example, consider the difference between a motivation to be correct versus a motivation to gain a reward. If we sincerely wanted to make a correct decision, we might do an exhaustive information search and expend plenty of time and cognitive energy on our decision making process. On the other hand, if what we are really interested in is gaining a reward, we might limit our information search and selectively attend to the information that supports the decision we really want. If you are motivated to do so, you could build an argument for a convertible Porsche 911 being a practical family car.

Marketers spend a great deal of time and money learning about the audience they are trying to reach. Markets can be segmented or divided into smaller, more manageable, and to some degree more homogenous groups by area, age, income, lifestyle, or myriad other factors. As technology advances, more personal ways of learning about the audiences for persuasive messages develop. For example, when you visit consumer web sites like Amazon.com, you're greeted by name. You are offered a list of suggested purchases based on your previous purchases and the clicks of your prior visits to the site compared to the behaviors and purchases of others who have visited the site. Bricks and mortar establishments have improved their ability to learn about the customers through technology, as well. Cameras in stores have allowed shopping scientists to discover trends in the way people shop. (Shoppers tend to drift to the right in countries where they drive on the right-hand side of the road and to the left in countries where they drive on the left-hand side.) The statistics on the average differences in the amount of time a man will spend in the store shopping alone, versus shopping with a woman, versus a woman shopping alone, have all been studied by shopping scientists.[13]

Companies can invest large amounts of money learning about their external audiences and how to influence them. Internal audiences can be less expensive to understand but just as vital. At some point in your career, you will probably attempt to understand your internal audiences through interviews, open meetings, surveys, or even water cooler chatter. Questionnaires can be useful for the purpose of understanding the attitudes and behaviors of people in your organization but only if the questionnaires are prepared well. (For help creating an effective questionnaire, see Appendix A.)

Personality factors can influence how your audience responds to your message. Although it may be difficult to know the personalities of the recipients of your message if you are giving a presentation to a large group, many of us work closely enough with people to know quite a bit about their individual personalities, including some things that may help us be more effective when we are attempting to influence them.

- **Intelligence.** A certain amount of intelligence will be required to understand and deeply process complex messages. However, the more intelligent your audience, the more likely it is they will spontaneously generate counter-arguments.

- **Self-monitoring.** We discussed the importance of self-monitoring for attitude behavior consistency. It's also important in determining the best frame for your message. Often people high in self-monitoring will respond better to a social framing of a message. In other words, they will be more swayed by arguments that target a social-adjustive attitude function or focus on what the message means for their relationships.
- **Authoritarianism or dogmatism.** People high in authoritarianism or dogmatism are very conscious of rules, order, hierarchy, and the way things are supposed to be. They tend to be close-minded and resistant. If you are trying to persuade someone who is high in authoritarianism or dogmatism, prepare your argument carefully and frame it in a way that they will find motivating, for example, the "being a good soldier" approach.
- **Need for cognition.** People who genuinely like to do a lot of mental work, who seek out complex problems, and who deliberate thoughtfully purely because they enjoy it, are high in the need for cognition. People high in this variable are likely to do central route processing, and even when the issues are not ego-involving, they simple enjoy the process. If you're attempting to influence a person high in the need for cognition, make certain your argument is carefully thought through.

It's critical to consider how you expect your audience to react to your message, with what emotional intensity and with what sort of bias. You can do a little information gathering ahead of time on this topic. Talk to people privately to get a sense of what reaction to anticipate. Know what they are expecting from you as well.

Perhaps the biggest challenge for persuaders to overcome is to understand how their audience will make a decision. Although we may tell ourselves that we are rational beings and our decisions are based on thoughtful deliberation of the evidence, that is often not the case. As we will see in Chapter 4, people make bad decisions, and even good decisions, for all sorts of reasons that might not have to do with evidence or logical reasoning. To be effective, you need to understand how your audience generally makes decisions and how they are liable to make a decision about your specific argument:

- Do they like statistics?
- Do they like details or just the facts?
- Do the like risk or "tried and true" solutions?
- Do they make decisions quickly?
- Do the want to know every possible scenario before they make a decision?
- Are they natural skeptics?
- Will their world view be challenged by what you are saying?
- Will they become defensive?
- Do they want to know what other people they respect have done?
- Do they want to know what other organizations are doing?

FROM THE RIGHT PERSON

Whom do you find to be credible? What makes a person credible? These may seem like easy questions at first, but if we think more deeply about them, we can see that they can be complex questions, yielding many different answers. For example, you may consider your parents to be credible people because you know they have your best interest at heart and you trust them. But if you were sick, would you go to them for advice? You'd go to your doctor, right? (Unless one or both of your parents are doctors, of course.) So, you find your doctor credible, but if you wanted to buy a computer, would you ask your doctor's advice? You might get better information from a person who sells computers because that person would be aware of the latest and greatest technology. But does this knowledge alone make him or her credible? Do you think the salesperson has your best interest at heart? If not, can you trust this person?

Credibility—or what Aristotle might call *ethos*—is not a single dimension. It has different, independent components. Furthermore, credibility is not an absolute truth. Credibility is assigned to others: It is not a property of those others. You may assign high credibility to a particular source, and your colleague may find that same source to be without credibility. Credibility is also context dependent. Your doctor is credible when it comes to your health, but that doesn't mean he or she knows about computers. People can have high credibility in some areas and not in others. Finally, credibility is not static. It can change over time. If your investments broker retires, he or she may not be a credible source of investment advice after a few years.

- **Expertise.** A person's knowledge or expertise can make them a credible source for information. We may trust the person's knowledge and ability.
- **Likability.** We find people we like to be more credible, even if we don't actually know them. Social attractiveness or charm can lend to their credibility.
- **Similarity.** We find people with whom we have something in common to be more credible. People who share our values or our beliefs are more likely to see things the way we would.
- **Goodwill.** We are more likely to extend credibility to people who demonstrate their goodwill toward others. If we perceive that people are only looking out for themselves, that can diminish their credibility.
- **Social skill.** People who are good communicators and have good interpersonal skills are perceived as more credible. A brilliant person who stumbles over words, fidgets, and doesn't make eye contact will lose credibility despite the intelligence of the argument being made.
- **Trustworthiness.** We are more likely to find people we trust credible, especially if we trust that the person doesn't have a hidden agenda when dealing with us. Trust, like credibility, has different components. We can trust in someone's ability, which is different from trusting in someone's loyalty or trusting in someone's honesty. At the very minimum, your audience needs to trust you enough to believe they can consider what you are saying, without worrying that you will take advantage of them to meet your own ends.

If you don't have any credibility, you need to acquire some—the sooner the better. Robert Gass and John Seiter, authors of *Persuasion, Social Influence and Compliance Gaining,* offer some suggestions for improving credibility.[14]

The Sleeper Effect

Have you ever remembered something you heard, but couldn't remember where you heard it? Messages can become separated from the source in memory over time, leading messages from high credibility sources to lose their advantage and messages from low credibility sources to lose their disadvantage. When this happens, it is called the sleeper effect. The research on the sleeper effect has demonstrated mixed findings that are far from robust. Sometimes the sleeper effect occurs, sometimes both messages from low credibility sources lose effectiveness, and sometimes the message and the source stay associated in memory. What this means is that as a persuader, you certainly can't plan on the sleeper effect happening. However, because it *can* happen, as a consumer of persuasive messages, you are wise to ask the person making the argument for his or her source. If he or she responds with something like, "Well, I know I read that somewhere, but I can't remember where" you know to be cautious. The message could be from a noncredible source.

Source: G. T. Kumkale and D. Albarracin, "The Sleeper Effect in Persuasion: A Meta-Analytic Review," *Psychological Bulletin*, 130, 1, (2004): 143–172.

- **Be prepared.** Know what you are talking about and be able to answer questions. Nothing shatters your credibility faster than knowing less about your argument than your audience.
- **Cite evidence and sources.** Research shows that when the source for evidence is cited, the argument is perceived as more credible.[15] This makes sense, whether you are dealing with people processing centrally or peripherally. The sources can serve as a peripheral cue for people using shallow processing. People thinking critically about your argument will want to know where your support came from, so they can determine its quality.
- **Share your credentials.** If you have credentials that lend to your expertise in an area, make that known up front. They won't do you any good if no one knows about them. Knowing about your credentials could have an impact on how your audience will process the rest of your message.
- **Build trust and display goodwill.** It's never a bad idea to treat people well. Your history with your audience will be a factor in their assessment of your trustworthiness and ultimately your credibility. If you have demonstrated your trustworthiness and goodwill toward your audience in the past, it will help their current judgment of you be more favorable. A history of prior success can make your job as a persuader much easier. If you haven't really had any dealings with the audience in the past, take the opportunity to build their trust and take the first steps toward building a good track record. Meet one-on-one with the people you are trying to persuade.
- **Engage the help of an already trusted source.** If your audience doesn't know you very well, you can increase the trust your audience feels toward you if you have an already trusted source introduce you or show his or her approval of you. Experts in the organization can be used to support your position. Hire a consultant.

For individuals and for organizations, credibility can be the cue the audiences uses to accept a message, it can be what causes the skeptic to give a persuader the benefit of the doubt, it is a weight that helps to keep the scale balanced in a time of crisis when integrity may be questioned. But good reputations are easily lost. Is an honest person still honest after telling a lie? One lie can make an honest person dishonest, but a thousand truths can't make a liar an honest man. Credibility is a prized but fragile force: Guard it. Grow it. You need it.

DISCUSSION QUESTIONS

1. Lance Armstrong's yellow LIVESTRONG wristbands started appearing on wrists all over the country a few years ago. Now you can see similar wristbands in various colors representing various causes (e.g., pink = Breast Cancer Awareness, white = Make Poverty History campaign). Today some colored wrist bands just represent sports teams or a product (the Indianapolis Colts offer bands in a variety of colors, including blue and white). How do the principles of influence we have discussed in this chapter explain people's attitudes toward the wristbands and the growth in their popularity? What do you predict for the future for their popularity?

2. Joe is staunchly opposed to human cloning. Ann would like to change his attitude on the matter to see cloning in a more favorable way. How would you introduce Ann to Social Judgment Theory and help her apply it to her persuasive efforts with Joe?

3. Jill (who is very interested in her appearance) and Jack read an article by a beautiful woman and respected beauty expert arguing that to keep skin "soft and ladylike," people should use her beauty products. The beauty expert had a number of really poor arguments. According to the Elaboration Likelihood Model (ELM), what sort of attitude change would you most likely expect in Jack and Jill?

ENDNOTES

1. M. Fishbein and I. Ajzen, *Belief, Attitude, Intention and Behavior: An Introduction to Theory and Research.* (Reading, MA: Addison-Wesley, 1975.)

2. D. J. Bem, D. J. (1972) "Self-perception theory," In L. Berkowitz (ed), *Advances in Experimental Social Psychology* (New York: Academic Press, 1972): 1–62.

3. D. Katz, "The Functional Approach to Attitudes," *Public Opinion Quarterly* 24 (1960): 163–204.

4. M. B. Smith, J. S. Bruner, and R. W. White, *Opinions and Personality* (New York: John Wiley, 1956).

5. R. T. LaPiere, "Attitudes vs. Actions," *Social Forces* 13 (1934): 230–237.

6. M. Snyder, "Self-monitoring of Expressive Behavior," *Journal of Personality and Social Psychology* 30 (1974): 526–537.

7. I. Ajzen, *Theory of Planned Behavior,* available at http://www.people.umass.edu/aizen/tpb.html. Date accessed 01/26/2006.

8. R. E. Petty and J. T. Cacioppo, "Issue Involvement as a Moderator of the Effects on Attitude of Advertising Content and Context," *Advances in Consumer Research,* 8 (1981): 20–24.

9. R. B. Zajonc, "Attitudinal Effects of Mere Exposure," *Journal of Personality and Social Psychology* 9, 2 (1968): 1–27.

10. W. C. Booth, G. G. Colomb, and J. M. Williams, *The Craft of Research* (Chicago: University of Chicago Press, 1995).

11. R. Levine, *The Power of Persuasion: How We're Bought and Sold,* (Hoboken, New Jersey: John Wiley & Sons, 2003): 113–135.

12. M. Sherif and C. I. Hovland, *Social Judgment: Assimilation and Contrast Effects in Communication and Attitude Change.* (Oxford, England: Yale University Press, 1961.)

13. Levine, *supra* n. 11: 25–28.

14. R. H. Gass and J. S. Seiter, *Persuasion, Social Influence, and Compliance Gaining,* 3rd ed. (Boston: Pearson Education, Inc., 2007): 74–93.

15. J. C. Reinard, "The Empirical Study of the Persuasive Effects of Evidence: the Status After Fifty Years of Research," *Human Communication Research* 15, 1 (1988): 3–59.

CHAPTER
4   THE EMOTIONAL SIDE OF PERSUASION

If you are delivering a message your audience has an inherent interest in or that is about something which affects them directly in an obvious and important way, lucky you! If not, you will need to engage their interest. So, how do you engage the interest of an otherwise uninterested audience and hold their interest through your message? Emotion. The emotional or psychological appeal of a message can serve as an attention getter, an attention holder, a motivation for action, and a peripheral cue. People are often influenced by their emotional response to a message, sometimes to the exclusion of logic and evidence.

Imagine this curious situation: An article in a city newspaper tells the story of a suburban woman who received a message from another planet stating that her small town was going to be destroyed by flood. The woman, a Mrs. Keech, received a message through automatic writing, sent to her from superior beings from a planet called "Clarion." The beings have visited the earth and have noticed fault lines in the earth's crust that foretell of the flood. The flood will create an inland sea spanning from the Arctic Circle to the Gulf of Mexico. All this will begin just before dawn on December 21st.

Mrs. Keech had been receiving messages for about nine months and had been asked by the beings to act as their representative to warn the people of Earth about the flood. By September, she had developed a small following. Among them was a physician from a nearby college town who had spread to word to a number of students with whom he met at his home for a discussion group. As the months passed, the groups regularly met to plan for the cataclysm. Some of the group members quit their jobs, some gave away possessions.

Late on the morning of December 20th, Mrs. Keech received a message telling her to ready her group for a visitor who would come to her house at midnight and escort the group to a flying saucer that would take them away to a safe place. The followers assembled at her house, and as midnight approached, the group was tense and silent, the ticking of the clock the only sound. Ten minutes to midnight. Five minutes to midnight. One minute. And then the twelve chimes of midnight sounded and ended. The believers sat and waited. And waited. Nothing happened.

Gradually the group began to re-examine the messages sent from Clarion, looking for an answer, but none seemed satisfactory. They began to lose composure. But, about 4:45 a.m., Mrs. Keech called for everyone's attention and announced that she had received another message. The message said that the faith of the group sitting there through the night had inspired God to call off the cataclysm and save the world. Mrs. Keech was also told that she should publicize the explanation to spread the word. For the rest of the day, members of the group, who had never contacted the media before, spoke to reporters and proselytized enthusiastically.[1]

In this case, with all the evidence to the contrary, Mrs. Keech's followers refused to give up their beliefs. In fact, they seemed to emerge from exposure to contradictory evidence even more committed than before. When a belief is held with deep conviction and commitment, and a person has taken some important action based on the belief that may be difficult to undo, an individual's belief can be strengthened despite exposure to evidence that plainly refutes it. Clearly, this was an emotional and psychological reaction, and therefore understandable in that light. From a psychological standpoint, it would be incredibly difficult to reconcile the act of quitting a job or giving away possessions with being wrong about a religious leader.

Emotion can be a powerful tool of social influence, and effective persuaders know that and use it. At the very minimum, it can motivate your audience to attend to your message. An emotional reaction to a psychological appeal can certainly serve as a peripheral cue. Other times, the emotional or psychological aspect of the appeal is designed to create a particular emotional reaction, and then other aspects of the message direct you toward an action to resolve the emotion.

Advertisements offer great examples through a plethora of psychological appeals. It makes sense, given a television or radio commercial will typically last only 15 to 20 seconds, and a print ad has to break through the clutter of all the other messages without even making a sound. Engaging the audience's emotion is one way to get a quick reaction.

Psychological appeals in advertising operate in several ways. They either assume you have and are aware of a need that the appeal will address, or they point out a need you didn't realize you had, or they create a need that previously you didn't have. Think about anything you enjoy, anything you wish for, anything that feels good. Or think about anything you fear, anything you would be embarrassed by, anything you would prefer to avoid. If you listed all those thoughts, they would represent a set of underlying psychological needs, and all of them would no doubt have been the basis for an advertisement.

For example, let's say you started your list with something you enjoy—going on vacation. What psychological need does that represent? It could be the need for fun, the need for adventure, or just the need for escape. Have those needs been used as the basis for any advertisements you can think of? How about, "Calgon, take me away!" See, you don't really need a vacation, you just need to buy some bath salts and everything will be much better.

You must use the right appeal for your audience. Take the success of the "Don't mess with Texas" anti-littering campaign. The campaign rallied Texas pride by featuring Texas favorites like Stevie Ray Vaughan and Willie Nelson in public service announcements telling Texans not to litter. It's hard to be certain the exact effectiveness of the ads because there is no way to control for other variables, but every time a visible litter study is done by the state, the amount of litter has decreased.[2] What a cute little owl encouraging people to "Give a Hoot. Don't Pollute" and a crying Native American weren't able to do, the "Don't mess with Texas" campaign did by hitting just the right emotional chord with the audience.

Using vivid language and telling stories injects an emotional quality into arguments. Some of the most influential figures throughout history have been the very best story tellers. People love stories; they become curious and engaged by stories. People pay attention to stories because, with the exception of the very worst stories, people want to know how the story will end. People can very quickly become emotionally invested in the characters of a story. Stories are able to simplify and communicate complex lessons that can generalize to other parts of life. Stories can capture and impart a vision. Presenting your message as a story is a way to infuse it with emotion. Being a *good* storyteller will make you more influential. To become a better storyteller:

- **Open with a hook.** Start the story with something that makes your audience so they want to find out more. Create an information gap that only your story can fill. "I worked for a company that changed ownership, and no one could have predicted what happened."
- **Don't get bogged down with details that aren't relevant to the story.** Spending a lot of time describing a place, what someone was wearing, or the weather is not going to add value, unless these details are integral to the story.
- **Use descriptive words, metaphor, simile or analogy.** Compare "The dog was in the parking lot" to "An enormous, sinister-looking black dog was lurking in the parking lot, which was totally empty except for my car."
- **Know your point and make the length of the story appropriate for the point.** A very long story to make a very minor point has little impact and will leave the audience wanting.

- **Feel emotions yourself.** When you tell a story, you feel some genuine emotion as you tell. Good stories tellers usually enjoy telling stories. Passionate storytellers get excited about their stories. Your genuine emotion will be felt by your audience.
- **Relate the story to your audience.** Make sure to let the audience know, if it isn't obvious, why the story is meaningful for them. A story can be engaging, even if it is pure entertainment, but generally as agents of influence, our stories will be more than that.

An image can create an emotional response even faster than a concise story. An attractive model, a cute puppy, or a sad, hungry-looking child will all arouse some sort of emotional response. So will a well-tailored suit and a good haircut. Visuals matter. Beyond arousing emotion, images can be convincing because of the ability to show evidence of an event, like the images that accompany news stories. Images, like graphs or flowcharts, can simplify difficult messages. Images can help people realize concepts that are otherwise difficult to grasp, like images of the AIDS quilt or the Vietnam War Memorial that convey the enormity of loss. Images, through icons, can create messages that are easy to remember. Images can present proof that something works, like before and after pictures for fitness equipment. But, of course, images can lie.

Sounds can also arouse emotion. A crying baby, the siren on a fire engine, even the doorbell will create an emotional reaction, but probably no sound more than the sound of music. Can music make you happy? Can it make you work harder? Shop longer? Spend more? Almost every restaurant or retail facility has music playing in the background. Research shows that people will take longer in stores and restaurants when music is of a slower tempo.[3] This leads to buying more items in retail establishments and ordering more drinks in restaurants. You'll notice that in many restaurants, where the goal is to turn the tables quickly, the music is a bit more up tempo.

The persuasiveness of music can be as simple as the positive associations that can form between music that makes you feel good and something else. Hook lines in jingles can be inadvertently committed to memory, then be easily recognized or brought to mind, helping us recognize products and reinforcing or reminding us of the positive association.

Music can serve as a peripheral cue. For example, the song you loved as a teenager might now be the background music for an automobile ad. On the other hand, music can sometimes contain lyrics that lead people to think and reflect on the message of the song. In some cases, music makes an argument that is centrally processed and can be persuasive.

SHOCK AND HUMOR APPEALS

Shock appeals are sometimes designed to do little more than get attention and cause an emotional reaction. Shock ads feature something unexpected that jolts the audience. Volkswagon's "Safe Happens" campaign includes shock ads. In one ad, friends are riding in their VW Jetta, chatting about a movie they've just seen and out of nowhere the car is smashed into by another vehicle. The accident is unexpected and gets the attention of the audience. Afterward we see the people who were in the car standing outside it visibly shaken but seemingly unharmed despite the damage to the car. The point of the message is the safety of the vehicle when the unexpected happens.

The very nature of shock ads requires edginess, but the ads are often criticized for going too far and being offensive. The United Colors of Benetton, a clothing brand of the Benetton Group headquartered in Ponzano, Italy, has received a great deal of notoriety in the press and in marketing classes, for several of their campaigns that featured shock ads. Luciano Benetton, one of the four Benetton family members who founded the Benetton group in 1965, argued that advertising wasn't just about selling more product but was a way to promote conversation and create social change. His method of attempting this was through a series of shock ads for Benetton. Luciano collaborated for 18 years with photographer Oliviero Toscani and gave him carte blanche for his photographs. Under Toscani, Benetton ads featured photos of a dying AIDS patient, and a nun and priest engaged in a kiss, among other images.

These print ads, which didn't feature any articles of Benetton clothing, caused some complaints. Perhaps the campaign that caused the loudest uproar was the "We, on Death Row" campaign which featured death row inmates. Photographs of 26 death row inmates appeared in magazines, billboards, and a 96-page catalog. The ads didn't mention the murdered victims but gave what many considered a sympathetic view of the murderers. The families of the murder victims did not respond with sympathy. Toscani, opposed to the death penalty, argued, "I just wanted to discuss the fact that they were waiting to be killed by a cold-blooded system."[4]

The value of shock ads lies in their ability to break through the clutter of messages and capture attention. However, they hold an inherent danger. The audience's comfort zone must be pushed in order to be shocking, but it can be pushed too far. You can actually be dismissed by an audience when you offend—rather than shock—them.

Another means of getting attention is with humor. Speakers often use humor in their opening remarks. Humor appeals are immensely popular in advertisements, and with good reason. If you were to think of your favorite commercial, to the extent that you have one, it would probably be an ad that involves humor.

Humor in an appeal can function other ways than just an attention getter. It can serve as a peripheral cue. "This is funny and I'm feeling good. I think I'll go along with this message." It can lead to a positive feeling being associated with the subject of a message, such as a product, through a process called classical conditioning. Yes, Ivan Pavlov and his famous dog research is what we're referring to here. As you may recall, Dr. Pavlov rang a bell right before delivering a blast of meat powder in the mouth of his dogs. After a while, the dogs came to associate the sound of the bell with the meat powder and would begin to salivate when they heard the bell even before they got any meat powder. Similarly, when we are exposed to a product and a humorous, feel-good message, we may associate the product with the good feeling. Later, when we're in a retail store, we might respond to exposure to the product with a good feeling, which of course will then lead us to purchase that product.

Humor appeals have their benefits, but as with shock appeals, there are caveats for using humor in your message. One concern is that the humor can become a distraction. People may remember the humor, but not the real message or product you were trying to get across.

Another caution is that humor may seem inappropriate to some audience members when the real message is a serious one. Jean Kilbourne is well known for her work exploring the depiction of women in advertising. She has made three films, *Killing Us Softly, Still Killing Us Softly*, and *Killing Us Softly III* that show her giving a talk to a live audience and presenting examples of advertisements that objectify women. Her main argument is that the depiction of women in advertising leads to a cultural objectification of women and an acceptance of violence against them. Periodically in her presentation, she uses humor, and it goes well with her live audience, always producing audible laughter. However, undergraduate college students viewing the videos frequently comment that her use of humor made them think of her as less credible and to wonder if she really thought the issue was all that serious. The key here is to make sure you understand your audience and how they will view your humor.

One final caution on the use of humor in your message. If you aren't funny, don't attempt the humor appeal. Attempts at humor that fall flat can damage your credibility and can be irritating to the audience.

FEAR APPEALS

Fear is another emotion frequently tapped in persuasive appeals. Like shock and humor, fear can be an attention-getter. Fear appeals have been used frequently in public health messages and, perhaps because of this, have been researched more than the other types of emotional appeals. Not smoking or quitting smoking, practicing safe sex, avoiding driving drunk, saying no to drugs, all of these issues have been to subject of fear appeals. The basic principle behind fear appeals is pretty simple: Scare people into changing. Does it work? Well, it's not as simple as the principle implies, but in general the more you are able to make people feel fear, the more likely you will persuade. That said, let's discuss some reasons why it's not that simple.

In order for fear appeals to be effective, they must do several things. First, the message must arouse a feeling of vulnerability to the fear. This could happen by bringing attention to the fact a risk exists, which could be a fact they already know, but don't believe applies to them. The challenge comes in making them believe that they are vulnerable to the risk. Creating a sense of vulnerability can be challenging and requires careful consideration of the audience. Smoking is a good example, especially for young people. Most people agree without too much debate that smoking is harmful to one's health. However, many young smokers are very good at exempting themselves from being vulnerable to this risk. *Yes, it's harmful, but I'll quit before it really does anything to me.* Young people feel especially invulnerable to the risks of smoking because the greatest risks are for long term health consequences, and it is easy for a young person to distance him or herself from those.

A fear appeal might need to inform the audience of a risk of which they were not aware. To be effective, they must believe that the threat you are referring to is real and that they are vulnerable to it. Take for example, messages about cooking ground beef to a certain internal temperature to kill bacteria. Today, even restaurant menus will inform patrons that undercooked ground beef can present health hazards. Years ago, before cases of illness caused by the e-coli bacteria made the headlines, many people were unaware of this danger. Highly publicized cases, like the Jack in the Box incident in 1993 when three Washington state children died after eating hamburgers contaminated with the bacteria, hit the news and talk shows and successfully persuaded people to believe in their vulnerability to this risk.

In addition to presenting a real threat that the audience feels vulnerable to, an effective fear appeal must offer something that the audience can do about this threat. The fear appeal must offer a solution that will be effective and one the audience believes they can actually do. Consider smoking again. Today, many of the messages targeting smokers don't focus on the dangers of smoking. That point doesn't need to be argued anymore, at least with adults. The messages don't focus on what the answer to the risk is. (How can you protect yourself from the dangers of smoking? Quit.) Instead, the ads focus on the real stumbling block for many people trying to quit, quitting aids to help them with their lack of ability to quit on their own. People know the dangers, they know the solution, but they don't know if they can implement the solution. This is where the patch, the gum, or the prescription come in, and this is what the advertisements offer.

The best fear appeals offer clear and specific suggestions for what do to do to protect oneself from risk. One straightforward fear appeal is a print ad for State Farm Insurance. It shows the interior of a nice apartment with an attractive rug on the floor and what appears to be a pair of expensive lady's shoes sitting on the rug. In the background, through an open door, a bathtub with water overflowing can be seen. The caption below asks, "You do have renters insurance, right?" The ad goes on to inform the readers that in an apartment, their belongings are not covered by the insurance carried by the property owner. The ad lets the readers know that for about the "price of one CD a month" they could be covered, and they can make that happen by contacting State Farm. This message lets readers know what they need to do and that they can do this effectively because it doesn't cost much money.

Fear appeals that offer an effective solution the audience perceives as doable are likely to elicit a response called "danger control" where the audience focuses on the solution to the threat. On the other hand, if a fear appeal presents no effective solution or presents a solution the audience doesn't feel capable of implementing, the response elicited will be one of "fear control." With fear control, the focus is on reducing the fear, rather than solving the problem. The person may put effort into staying calm instead of dealing with the threat, because no effective means has been presented. Fear control can lead to defeatist behaviors such as denial or panic. One print ad targeting parents, for example, shows a burly looking, middle-aged man sitting at his home computer and the caption reads, "Meet your daughter's new best friend, Becky." The fear of online predators is easily aroused in most parents, and this ad does that effectively. What it doesn't do, however, is give parents specific suggestions on what to do to protect their children. It does tell parents to report inappropriate or suspicious activity, but by the time there is something to report, some damage may have already been done.

COGNITIVE DISSONANCE

What is an issue you feel strongly about? AIDS in Africa? Fighting hunger? Domestic violence? Teen pregnancy? Think about the social problems of our time and make a mental note of the ones that you think are the most serious and urgent. Have you selected at least three?

Now, for each of those issues you indicated are the most serious and urgent of our time, can you describe what you did today to help? How about this week? This month?

Are you starting to feel bad about this? Starting to wonder how important you really think these issues are if you haven't done much to help? Good! Then this little exercise worked. The goal of this exercise is to introduce you to the theory of cognitive dissonance.

Cognitive dissonance occurs whenever two cognitions are in disharmony. Cognitions are simply mental representations. Any mental representation of information is a cognition. Your beliefs, values, and attitudes are cognitions; your knowledge of your own behaviors are cognitions. Relationships between cognitions can be irrelevant (I like ice cream. I've been to Spain.), harmonious (I value organization. I hired a professional organizer.) or dissonant when they contradict or don't completely agree with each other in some way. For example, let's say you have promised yourself you would cut down on your calories in your effort to be fit. Let's say you have also just completed a very rich Italian meal: Some chicken scaloppini, some bread with herbed olive oil, a salad with creamy Parmesan dressing, and a serving of tiramisu to top it off. When you think about your commitment to keep your calorie intake low and the meal you just consumed, you may initially have some difficulty reconciling those dissonant two cognitions. That is cognitive dissonance.

The theory of cognitive dissonance states that dissonant cognitions will create an unpleasant state of tension and you will be motivated to reduce that tension. You can reduce the tension in a number of ways:[5]

1. **Deny the cognition.** If you are able to believe that one of the cognitions is false or incorrect, you will feel better. In our example, you might be able to convince yourself that none of what you ate was rich in calories. Or, perhaps you might convince yourself that the portions were so small that the caloric intake couldn't have been that high.

2. **Downplay the importance of the cognition.** Here you diminish the importance of what you think. The cognition may be true, and you accept that, but you think it doesn't really matter. You might say that consuming a large number of calories once in a while isn't a problem.

3. **Reduce your level of choice.** Here you make it seem as if you really didn't have much choice in the matter: Something forced you. You might say, "I was out to dinner with one of our biggest clients who happens to be a big eater. What was I going to do? Order a salad? That wouldn't have been very good for our relationship."

4. **Add new cognitions.** You may be able to find new information to add to the mix that will somehow allow the cognitions to exist harmoniously. For our example, you might remember an article you read that suggested eating too little can send your body into "starvation mode" leading it to store calories and slow weight loss. By eating an occasional large meal, you could prevent your body from going into starvation mode.

5. **Change your belief, attitude, or behavior.** You can change yourself in a way that creates consonance between the cognitions. In our example, you might change your behavior and give up your afternoon snack for a week to make up for the night out. Or you might change your attitude and decide you don't really want to lose weight after all.

Cognitive dissonance is used by persuaders in two ways. It can be created by a message, and then the way to relieve it can be suggested. For example, in a print advertisement for Chevy Silverado, readers are asked if their truck has a variety of features and capabilities. This is followed by the question: "Did you buy the right truck?" The intent here is clearly to cause buyer's remorse, in other words, to make readers question and ultimately regret the purchase of their truck if it was not a Silverado. If the buyer experiences remorse, the solution is also clear. Next time, buy a Silverado.

Another way that persuaders use cognitive dissonance is to assume it already exists in the audience and to offer them a way of reducing the dissonance. For example, a print ad for Dove ice cream bars shows a delicious looking bar being pulled from a pool of rich, creamy chocolate. Underneath the image is the line, "For the love of Dove, treat yourself." This advertisement works on the assumption that the image will make the readers want a Dove bar, but the readers might think they shouldn't have one, creating dissonance. How does the ad help reduce dissonance? It offers a way to diminish the importance. You are "treating" yourself. A "treat" suggests that you will consume the occasional Dove bar, and there's nothing wrong with the occasional sweet treat. Of course later, after purchasing a box of Dove bars, one might have to deal with dissonance aroused by consuming the entire box within a few days, but that's a different story.

The classic study on cognitive dissonance focuses on changing attitudes to relieve dissonance.[6] Subjects for this study were students in a course that required them to participate in psychology experiments for a certain number of hours. At some time during the course, it was announced that for some studies, participants would be interviewed about the experiment because the psychology department was trying to evaluate experiments to improve them in the future. In reality, only participants in dissonance study would be interviewed, and the interview was a critical part of the study. Nevertheless, this announcement created the sense in the participants that the interviews were unrelated and that would lead them to be more open in there answers.

For the experiment, subjects were asked to work on a very boring task, such as putting spools on a tray until the tray was full, then emptying the tray and putting the spools back on, or turning wooden pegs just a quarter of a turn, over and over and over again.

Participants in the study were assigned to one of three experimental conditions. For every condition, participants had to spend an agonizingly long period of time on the tedious tasks, but after the tasks were completed one of three things would happen. In the first condition, the participants were simply asked to participate in the "interview for the psychology department" and permitted to leave.

In the second condition, participants were asked if they could do the experimenter a favor. They were told that a student was waiting to begin the experiment, and they were asked if, while they were waiting to be interviewed for the psychology department, they would be willing to tell the student that the experiment was really fun and would be enjoyed. In return for the favor, the experimenter would give them a dollar.

In the third condition, participants were asked to do the favor of lying to the unsuspecting student waiting to begin the experiment, but in return for the favor were given twenty dollars. This study was conducted in 1957, by the way, so twenty dollars was a significant chunk of change.

After telling the waiting student, who was actually a confederate working for the experimenter, the lie about the experiment, participants completed the interview that was ostensibly for the psychology department. The interview included a question asking the students to rate if the experiment was interesting and enjoyable on a scale of –5 (extremely dull and boring) to +5 (very exciting and interesting).

The interesting question for the experiment is this: Did participants in the three different groups, who all completed the same boring tasks, differ in how interesting and enjoyable they found the experiment? The answer is, yes, but perhaps not in the way you might imagine. Intuitively, we might think the participants paid twenty dollars would give the experiment the highest rating. They got paid the most money and might be in a pretty good mood about the experiment because of their unexpected financial gain. However, the group giving the experiment the most favorable rating was actually the group receiving only a dollar.

Why would that be? The theory of cognitive dissonance can help us understand this finding. Let's ignore the control group for now. They didn't get paid any money and didn't get asked to tell a lie, and their negative ratings of the experiment reflected the true nature of the very boring tasks participants were asked to complete. Let's think about what might be going on in the mind of participants who were asked to lie. Lying to an unsuspecting student and creating false expectations is not a very nice thing to do, so how does a student deal with the two cognitions: Lying is wrong and I just told a lie? Will they experience cognitive dissonance? They will, unless they have what they consider to be sufficient justification for their actions. In this case, twenty dollars would seem sufficient. (I told a little lie, which is inconsistent with my beliefs, but I got paid a lot of money.) On the other hand, what can you do if you have no sufficient justification? (I told a lie, which is inconsistent with my beliefs, and I did that for only a dollar.)

This person is experiencing cognitive dissonance and will be motivated to reduce it, but their options for achieving that are somewhat limited. They can't undo their behavior; it's unrealistic for them to change their attitude toward one dollar and see that as justification; it's not likely they'll rethink their attitude toward lying (Maybe lying is okay after all), so what can they do? One way for them to reduce their dissonance is for them to change their attitude toward the tasks. (I think those tasks weren't so bad.) If they weren't so bad, then that wasn't really a lie. That explains why the ratings of the tasks were significantly more favorable in the one dollar group. In sum, they acted inconsistently with their beliefs without justification, producing dissonance, which they reduced through attitude change.

If you are hoping to change someone's attitude or behavior through cognitive dissonance, some conditions must be met. First, the person must actually feel some level of tension produced by the dissonant cognitions. It could be that we have dissonant cognitions that we just aren't thinking about at the moment, meaning we may not experience cognitive dissonance. If those dissonant cognitions are brought to mind, however, then we would experience the expected dissonance.

If tension is felt, creating attitude change requires the perception of a negative consequence and some perceived responsibility for that negative consequence. In the experiment, the negative consequence was the supposed expectations participants created in the unsuspecting student by their lie. Furthermore, the person must feel that they had some measure of choice in the behavior. If, for example, the subjects were told that in order to complete the experiment and meet their course requirement, they had to lie to the student, they wouldn't have experienced any attitude change.

Finally, the feeling of tension must be attributed to the cognitive dissonance and not something else. Let's say for example, the weather alert siren located right outside the psychology building was being serviced at the time a participant was completing the experiment. A loud siren blaring repeatedly might seem like a good reason to feel tense. If a participant misattributed the arousal from cognitive dissonance to the siren, no attitude change would take place.

PROPAGANDA TECHNIQUES: CREATING AN EMOTIONAL REACTION THROUGH BIAS AND EXAGGERATION

Propaganda is an attempt at persuasion that appeals to emotions, not reason. The propagandist appeal is typically a biased or selective version of the truth with the specific objective of shaping beliefs, attitudes, and behaviors. This objective is achieved through the deliberate distortion or omission of information, rather than an impartial, reasoned argument. Propaganda is an attempt to persuade that involves an intentional bias or exaggeration.

Emotionally loaded language.[7] Name calling wasn't allowed in elementary school, but it's a common propaganda technique for some adults. Name calling, labeling, and using loaded language are all ways that carefully chosen words can shape the response people will have to a message. Think about the mental reaction to different labels for groups of people. What happens when journalists are labeled the "media elite?" When environmentalists are called "tree huggers?" Social labels can have a positive or negative connotation, but the label has a meaning in our minds, and when the label is used, that meaning is activated. Propagandists are able to reap the emotional rewards of using labels.

Loaded words, like labels, have an emotional connection. They mean something more than objective words. Take for example the statement, "That was a naïve decision." Does that mean something more than, "That was a poor decision?" Yes, it certainly does. It says something negative about the decider as well as the decision. The decider isn't professionally mature, doesn't know what's going on, possibly can't be trusted with important decisions that may require more experience. Loaded language can be positive as well as negative. Consider PAAWS, the Pet Anti Aging Wellness System, which offers a "uniquely formulated, turbo-charged supplement regimen for your cats, packed into delicious, nutritional treats." A loaded word can pack quite an emotional punch.

The *glittering generality* is a positive use of loaded language where words that have positive emotional associations are used in a way that distorts or is simply not warranted. For example, nutritional supplements that are not regulated by the FDA are often marketed in ways that use the word "science" or are produced by companies that have the word "science" in their name. In our culture, we have a great respect for science and have a pretty good idea of what it means for something to be tested scientifically; however, many of these products use the word "science" in their marketing or in their name without ever actually saying that the products have been scientifically tested. They are able to benefit from the positive emotional association people have with science and scientifically proven effectiveness when it is not actually warranted.

Another effective word game is using euphemisms. A euphemism is a neutral or positive word used in place of a more negative word to blunt the effect of the word and make it whatever the word refers to more palatable. Downsizing, reorganizing, restructuring may all be euphemisms for firing a portion or laying-off employees.

Creating false connections.[8] A clever way of creating a false connection is putting together two images or an image with words so a connection is perceived but never stated. A good example of this is Apple Computer's "think different" campaign that included black and white photos of famous free-thinking historic figures, such as Mahatma Gandhi and Albert Einstein, accompanied by the Macintosh Apple icon with the tag line "think different." An association between the people in the ads and Apple is created by the images, even though the individuals obviously never used a Macintosh. (See Figure 4.1.)

Testimonials can be a propaganda technique that creates a false association when the person giving the testimonial isn't able to give qualified testimony. When an actor—who is not a doctor but plays one on TV—endorses a medication, that person is not any more knowledgeable about medicine than your neighbor or your Uncle Bert. Actors are associated with companies and brands often because of the parts they play, rather than any expertise they may have. For example, Sam Waterston, the actor appearing for many years in the fictional role of District Attorney Jack McCoy on the hit T. V. show *Law and Order*, has served as the spokesperson for TD Ameritrade. Despite the fact that Sam Waterston is a graduate of Yale University, a humanitarian activist, and has had a long, very successful career in film and on the stage, his invitation to be a spokesperson probably had more to do with his character's image of integrity, rather than his own personal image. People are much more likely to respond to his endorsements with an association to his character on *Law and Order* rather than anything they know about him personally.

Card stacking is another commonly used technique of propaganda. Card stacking refers to presenting a one-sided argument or selectively presenting only information that supports one side of an argument. This technique is most

Figure 4.1   Mahatma Gandhi, who died in 1948, with the old AppleComputer logo.

effective when the audience has no knowledge of the omitted information. For example, in a recent congressional election, an ad was aired accusing a candidate of not paying his business taxes. In reality, the taxes had not been paid, but the business referred to in the ad was a family business that the candidate had not been active in for many years.

Propaganda in advertising. Much of advertising is informative and reminds or informs consumers of new products or new features. Advertising that would be considered propaganda uses words or presents information in a way that purposely distorts reality. Propaganda in advertising is, unfortunately, quite widespread.

Advertisers will often carefully choose their words and cautiously construct their phrases in order to create certain impressions without actually making a direct statement. For example, a saying, "No pain reliever works faster than X" might create the impression that X works faster than other pain relievers, but of course that is not what is stated: Other pain relievers might very well work at the same speed as X. Saying, "Nothing is tougher on stains" might make a person think that the product being referred to offers some advantage over other products when it comes to being tough on stains. Even fear appeals can be considered propaganda when there isn't actually a legitimate threat to the audience. Advertisers use a number of familiar tactics to manipulate the perception of their audience.[9]

- **Weasel words.** Weasel words allow advertisers to weasel out of promises by implying things, without actually saying them. Words like "helps" or "virtually." Does something help prevent a cold or gingivitis or osteoporosis? Help is a very fuzzy word. What does it mean to say, "Works virtually overnight" or "Leaves your dishes virtually spotless."
- **The irrelevant claim.** A claim that has little to do with purpose of the product, but adds a touch of drama and suggests superiority. Coffeemate is "the original." Airborne (a cold medication) was "created by a school teacher."
- **The question claim.** Imply something through a question. *What could be better? Who could give you more? Why not buy the original? Is it love? Or is it Fancy Feast?* A print ad for Pegasus faucets asks, "Luxury is only for the privileged? What gave you that idea?"
- **The advantage claim.** The claim suggests an advantage over other products when, in fact, there is none. Breyers ice cream is made with "fresh milk" and "pure sugar." Bread is made with 100 percent wheat (that is not the same thing as 100% *whole* wheat). Hellmann's is made with eggs, oil, and vinegar, as is every other real mayonnaise.
- **The hazy claim.** An unsupported claim exploiting confusion. A Sonicare toothbrush ad begins, "Simplicity is knowing a healthy smile can lead to a healthy life." An ad for OxyClean stain fighter encourages you to "Double your detergent's whitening power." Carnation Instant Breakfast tells you, "Better mornings inspire even better days. So start with a moment that is all yours."
- **The magic ingredient claim.** Magic secret ingredients make the product a good choice. Spot Shot carpet cleaner is made with "4-D Cleaning Power." Actifade for age spots contains "powerful medication." Olay eye transforming cream contains VitaNiacin.
- **The ad as information.** Advertisers are skillful at disguising their persuasive efforts as helpful information. Infomercials are perhaps the best known form of this. A full half hour is spent telling you about the features and benefits of the product, giving you testimonials, and expert commentary. Then, a different announcer comes on to tell the price and how to order, making it seem like a commercial is occurring during an informational show.

Instead of, or in addition to, using the established tricks of advertising, many organizations are advertising in less traditional ways in an effort to build brand loyalty and establish lasting relationships with their customers. For example, USAA Insurance sends magazines to the children of their customers nearly from the time they are old enough to read. The magazines have stories and posters kids can take out and hang on their walls, and the magazines change as the kids get older to stay age-appropriate.

By the time the kids are looking to buy the own insurance, their relationship with USAA is already well established and long term. Gillette, in a smart marketing move, decided to send every male turning eighteen a free razor within a month of his birthday. Something free, a good product. A loyal customer, who only has to buy replacement blades.

PUTTING IT ALL TOGETHER

Japan lags behind other countries when it comes to women in the civilian labor force. A few decades ago, women played mostly supportive roles in the workplace. Many quit their jobs when they got married or had children, and their employers did little to encourage them to come back to work. But now, with a growing labor shortage that is only expected to get worse, Japanese companies are pursuing women employees.

Let's say you are the vice president of human resources for a Japanese company and you've been given the task of enticing Japanese women to work. So far, your company has agreed to offer part time hours for the first time, but that hasn't been very effective. What would you do? Where would you start?

You're first step is determining your influence goal. In this case you goal is to create true persuasion in the women because you want them to stay in the workforce and feel good about working again. If you know little about your audience, learning about them is the key. You could create a questionnaire, so you can learn about their attitudes toward returning to work. Learn what function their attitude toward work serves for them. Do they lack the knowledge needed to make the right decision for them? (Can I work part time? What if I need a day off for family obligations?) Does their attitude serve a value expressive function? (My family comes first.) Once you understand your audience, you will know how to frame your message in a way that targets what is important to them. When you know how to frame your message, you can decide the sort of support to use and what type of emotional element to include that will appeal to your audience's needs. Finally, you also need to consider what barriers prevent the women from doing what the company needs them to do and eliminate as many of these barriers as possible. (Is childcare a big concern? Could the company offer on-site daycare?)

Sweeping change isn't accomplished with a single message, at least not usually. As Shoko Kobayashi, manager of division promoting women at Mizuho Financial Group in Japan says, "It's not difficult to set up a [female-friendly] system." But he adds, "The hardest part is changing people's mentality. It takes a long time."[10] This type of change is created through a persuasive campaign, which is a concert of different messages delivered via different media with the same underlying point. The same core meaning is presented through a number of different and repeated messages. Public service announcements that seek to change social behaviors to protect the public and improve people's health are part of a campaign. For example "the Truth" anti big tobacco campaign features a number of different television commercials, billboards, and a web site. Creating change in the organization is no different. One presentation, one memo, one letter, is probably not going to create lasting, sweeping change.

Whether we are dealing with a persuasive campaign meant to create broad change, an inspiring speech by a visionary leader, the request for help by a peer, or a direct order given by an authority, effective social influence starts with a persuader who understands the recipient. As consumers of social influence, we need to understand our own motivation better than the people trying to influence us, so we can recognize moments when are reacting in a way that isn't in our best interest. We need to be critical consumers of persuasive messages when important decisions are being made. For us to be successful agents of influence, it doesn't matter what type of social influence we're employing; we need the same basic steps: Know what you want, motivate your audience, and make it easy for them.

DISCUSSION QUESTIONS

1. Think of an example of a fear appeal that succeeded in influencing you. What made the message effective?

2. You are a struggling student working hard to make financial ends meet. You can't afford to waste a dime, and yet you just went out and bought a very expensive watch. What are you likely to experience and what you do make yourself feel better?

3. Think of examples of advertisements using propaganda. What products are being advertised? Do some sorts of products tend to lend themselves more readily to advertisements using propaganda than others?

ENDNOTES

1. L. Festinger, H. W. Riecken, and S. Schacter, *When Prophecy Fails* (Minneapolis: University of Minnesota Press, 1956).
2. "Don't Mess with Texas. Real Texans Don't Litter" 2005 Visible Litter Results, available at http://www .dontmesswithtexas.org/about/research.php. Retrieved 7/19/2007.
3. R. E. Milliman, "The Influence of Background Music on the Behavior of Restaurant Patrons," *Journal of Consumer Research* 13(1986): 286–289.
4. CBS News, "Catalog of Killers," May 2000, available at http://www.cbsnews.com/stories/2000/05/30/60II/main200723.shtml. Retrieved 7/27/2007.
5. R. M. Perloff, *The Dynamics of Persuasion* (Hillsdale, New Jersey: Lawrence Erlbaum, 2002): 227.
6. L. Festinger, *A Theory of Cognitive Dissonance* (Stanford, California: Stanford University Press, 1957).
7. "Propaganda," available at http://www.propagandacritic.com/. Date accessed 8/03/2007.
8. *Ibid.*
9. C. Wrighter, *I Can Sell You Anything* (New York: Ballentine, 1972).
10. M. Inada, "Japanese Companies Woo Women Back to Work," *The Wall Street Journal* (July 23, 2007): B1, B3.

CREATING QUESTIONNAIRES

At some point in your professional career, if you haven't done this already, you will want to create a questionnaire. Questionnaires are useful tools for learning about people's beliefs, behaviors, and attitudes if, and only if, the questionnaires are well prepared. In the art of persuasion, questionnaires are a staple. They open the door to understanding your audience which, as we have stated repeatedly, is key.

Before you begin writing down questions, think long and hard about your purpose. What are you trying to learn and how are you going to use this information? Ask yourself the following questions:

1. How many times do I want to administer this questionnaire and to whom?

Let's say you are a human resources manager and you have a very general question about employees' attitudes toward work/life balance. You may want to have all employees complete your questionnaire just one time. That would be a cross-sectional survey and, as the name suggests, it will give you a cross section of information at one point in time. Perhaps, on the other hand, you are more interested in following the changes in expectations of newly hired employees regarding work/life balance. How many hours a week do they expect to work? Is that different from the number of hours people expected to work five years ago, or will expect to work a few years from now? If you are interested in learning how newer employees feel about work/life balance compared to next year or five years from now, you might give newly hired employees your questionnaire, and then again in one year or five, give the latest generation of newly hired employees the questionnaire. This is a survey with successive independent samples.

Your interest could be in how attitudes change over time for the same employee. You might ask the same employees to complete the questionnaire after being with the company for one year and then again after three years to see if there is a change in attitude over time. This is a longitudinal survey and can be over any length of time.

2. How will I administer my questionnaire?

You can administer questionnaires in writing, by phone, electronically, or by face-to-face interview. The best choice depends on your goals for the questionnaire and the nature of the questions. Obviously when people are identifiable, such as with face-to-face interviews, social desirability becomes an issue. In other words, people may not be completely honest because they may not want to answer questions in ways they think will make them look bad. In organizations, people may also fear the repercussions of answering questions honestly if their answers are negative toward the organization in some way.

The other side of the argument though is the need to explain questions or probe for further information. If someone is filling out a questionnaire in writing or online, generally there is no way to get clarification. How valuable is the data you've collected if the people filling out your questionnaire didn't understand what your questions were asking? Also, if your questionnaire is more exploratory in nature, you may ask open-ended questions and want to probe people for more information in a way you can't do unless you're interacting with the respondent:

Interviewer: Did you try product X?

Respondent: Yes.

Interviewer: Can you tell how you felt about it?

Respondent: I didn't like it.

Interviewer: Can you tell me a little more about that? Was there something in particular you didn't like?

3. What type of questions should be asked?

In general, there are two types of questions, open-ended and close-ended. Open-ended questions invite respondents to answer in their own words. Close-ended questions require only brief, restricted answers or give the respondents a set of fixed alternatives from which to select an answer. Open-ended questions allow respondents more freedom in their answer and may reveal information that the creator of the questionnaire was completely unaware of. Close-ended questions are more restricting, but the data collected is much easier to analyze, such as examining the percentage of people who responded "Yes" versus the percentage of people who responded "No" to a question. Open-ended questions may require a thoughtful sifting through the answers looking for themes that may be informative. They can be more subjective and much more labor-intensive.

CONSTRUCTING THE QUESTIONNAIRE

Nothing about surveying people is more frustrating, and embarrassing, than spending time, money, and other resources on administering a questionnaire, only to find out you haven't collected any useable data. Two things you can do to prevent this from happening are:

1. Before collecting any data, make sure you know exactly how you will analyze it. If you plan to use a particular statistical analysis or if you want to create certain types of graphs or charts, make sure the answers you collect will be in a form you can use.

2. Pretest your questionnaire on a few people who are similar to your target group and have no prior knowledge of the questionnaire's subject or purpose.

The following suggestions will help you create a more effective questionnaire:

- Ask innocuous questions first, personal questions last.
- Qualify early.
- Be aware of response set options. For example:

    Strongly Agree, Agree, Neutral, Disagree, Strongly Disagree

- Use plain English.
- Avoid leading questions.

    Rate your level of disapproval of television violence.

- Avoid obvious social desirability.

    Do you donate money to worthwhile causes?

- Avoid double-barreled questions.

    Rate your level of satisfaction with your current diet and exercise habits.

- Avoid negations.

   At parties, I do not attempt to say things that others will not like.

- Be sure sample has the requested information.

   How many times has your teenager consumed alcohol?

- Put conditional information prior to key idea.

   I frequently use foul language when I am really upset.

- Keep questions concise.
- Avoid irrelevant questions.
- Don't forget to pretest the questionnaire.

A NOTE ON SELECTING RESPONDENTS

You may choose to invite everyone in the population to complete your questionnaire, where population means everyone who could belong to the group of interest. So, if you have one hundred employees, and you ask all one hundred of them to complete your survey, you've included the entire population. On the other hand, let's say you have one thousand employees. You may want to survey all of them, but you may want to survey a smaller portion. Or let's say you are surveying customers and you have millions of them. You will need to select a sample to complete your survey. A number of different means of selecting a sample exist, all with the goal of balancing the best information with the practicalities involved in selecting the respondents.

Obviously, the best information comes from a representative sample. But how do you select a truly representative sample? Random selection might be the knee-jerk response for most of us, but in reality random selection can be tricky. It might be a very practical option when you are conducting an internal survey, but as soon as you move outside your organization, you run into trouble.

Let's say you have a great idea for a new product for teenagers. However, since you're not a teenage anymore and neither are your friends, you will want to survey some actual teenagers to get their reactions. Where do you get the magical list of all teenagers from which to select names randomly to use in your sample? Guess what? You can't get one of those as it simply doesn't exist. But what you can get is a list of high schools. You could randomly select high schools and then survey all the students at the selected high schools. This is known as cluster sampling and is sometimes much more practical than simple random sampling.

If you go with this option, you will lose kids who are home schooled or who have dropped out of school, or who are locked in juvenile centers, etc., but let's say you are willing to accept that. You're not out of the woods yet. You still have to get permission from the school to survey the students. If they do give you permission to access the students (let's say your great product is a newfangled study aid that the schools view as meritorious), there's still one more problem. In order to survey anyone under eighteen, the school will insist that you get parental permission (which ethically you should do regardless).

Our point is that selecting a representative sample is tough. You can begin to see why people are sometimes stopped and asked questions while walking through the mall. Is this representative? Not really. But it certainly is practical.

INDEX